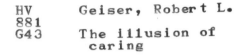

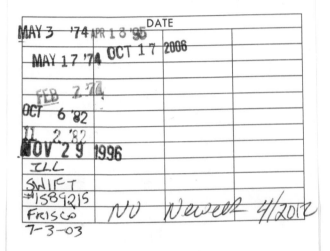

DATE			
MAY 3 '74 APR 1 3 '95			
MAY 17 '74 OCT 1 7 2006			
FEB 7 '74			
OCT 6 '82			
JL 2 '82			
NOV 2 9 1996			
ILL			
SWIFT #1589215			
FRISCO 7-3-03	NU Newell 4/2012		

The Illusion of Caring

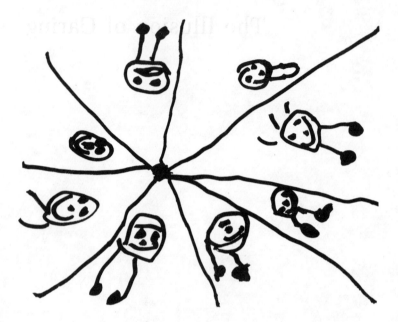

"A broken-up family" — six-year-old boy

The Illusion of Caring

Children in Foster Care

by Robert L. Geiser

Beacon Press   Boston

Beacon Press books are published under the auspices
of the Unitarian Universalist Association

Published simultaneously in Canada by Saunders of Toronto, Ltd.

Printed in the United States of America

9 8 7 6 5 4 3 2 1

Library of Congress Cataloging in Publication Data

Geiser, Robert L
  The illusion of caring: children in foster care.
  Includes bibliographical references.
  1. Foster home care—United States—Case studies.
I. Title.
HV881.G43   362.7'33'0973   73-6246
ISBN 0-8070-2378-7

The selections on pages 67–68 are reprinted by permission from
Momentum (February 1971), journal of the National Catholic
Education Association.

Contents

"I prefer the errors of enthusiasm to the indifference of wisdom, for a society that permits an excess of indifference needs more than anything else an excess of caring."

WHITNEY M. YOUNG, JR.

Introduction

This book is about some American families and their children. They are not the typical American family of television. The mother is not clever and oversolicitous of her family; the father is not a competent breadwinner, easily manipulated but lovable; and the children are not precocious and well scrubbed. Nor has the family been sanitized and neatly packaged inside a $40,000 suburban home. Unlike television, too, whose families never have any problems that can't be solved within thirty minutes (less time for multiple commercials), the families in this book haven't solved any of their problems. Nor are they likely to solve them. Since this is a book about the realities of life for many American families, it also differs from television in that there are no happy endings.

The families in this book all have one thing in common. They are unable to fulfill the family function of raising their own children. This book is especially about the 300,000 American children who were unable to live with their parents and were in foster care during 1970. If it is 1975 before you read this book, it will then be about 364,000 American children. That's only five out of a thousand children, which isn't too bad, really, unless you happen to be one of them.

Three-quarters of these children live with foster families and the remainder find homes in child care institutions. After they are placed, society will forget them until the placement collapses.

Then the child will be moved again . . .
and again . . .
and once more.

While society is indifferent to his needs, the child will fluctuate between hope and despair — hope that his family will reclaim him, despair when they don't. Society will provide him with the illusion of caring, but the child will eventually come to know the truth. He will know that he is one of the
orphans of the living.

"My family"

1

What Happened to My Parents?

"Daddy's away — a sad face"
"Daddy's home — a happy face"

"Home life is the highest and finest product of civilization. It is the greatest molding force of mind and character. Children should not be deprived of it except for urgent and compelling reasons." [1]

"It is hereby declared to be the policy of the Commonwealth to direct its efforts, first, to the strengthening and encouragement of family life for the protection and care of children; to assist and encourage the use by a family of all available resources to this end; and to provide substitute care of children only when the family itself . . . [is] unable to provide the necessary care and protection to insure the rights of any child to sound health and normal physical, mental, spiritual and moral development." [2]

It is generally accepted in our culture that the responsibilities of parents toward their children are to feed, clothe, and shelter them; to protect them against dangers in the environment; to see that they are educated; and to give them a "moral" upbringing that will make them sound and productive citizens. Society relies primarily upon the family to supervise the growth and development of children.

1

But sometimes families, like individuals, have difficulty functioning. Years ago, when our society wasn't so mobile, people often had relatives living nearby who could help them in times of crisis. Now, with at least one family in five moving each year, extended family members aren't so available to the nuclear family in times of crisis. Without support, some families, also like individuals, collapse under the pressures of living in our society.

While some families function efficiently most of the time and then break down in times of stress, other families never do function smoothly. It takes no special economic, educational, or mental health qualities to become a father or mother. However, raising children is another matter entirely. That process is guaranteed to highlight the flaws in all of us. Some parents never are able to meet their responsibilities to care for their children.

Whenever families break down or fail to function as expected in our society, child neglect is the inevitable result. Child neglect is the effect on a child of parental (or other caretaker's) inability to meet the child's needs adequately. Sometimes the neglect is so serious that the child has to be removed by society from the parents' care. For over 300,000 American children unable to live with their families, this is a reality.

Being rescued from parental neglect is only the beginning of their troubles. The services provided for these children by the state turn out to be a form of public neglect, an illusion of caring. It takes a while for the children in care to realize they have been doubly ill-treated. In the meantime, separated from their parents, they sit and try to puzzle out, "What happened to my parents that I had to leave them?"

REASONS FOR PLACEMENT

Studies of the reasons for placement of children in foster care[3] show that the majority of cases can be accounted for by five major factors. (When the children of a large child

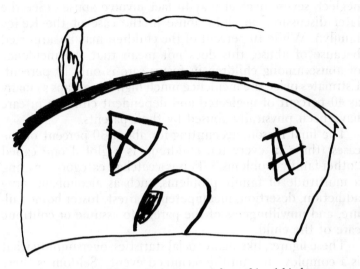

A seven-year-old boy in foster care drew this of his house

care institution in Massachusetts were classified under these categories, the resulting percentages were quite similar to the studies.) The figures to be cited are probably fairly typical of the situation throughout the United States.

About 30 percent of the children who come into foster care do so because of the physical illness of the adult (mother, father, foster parent, or other caretaker). This is about three children out of every ten admitted into care.

A special form of illness, mental illness of the mother, is responsible for another 15 percent of the admissions, or about one and a half children out of every ten.

The child's own emotional or personality problems, making him unmanageable or unacceptable to the parents, account for another 15 percent of the cases in care. Again, this is one and a half children in every ten.

About one child in ten, or 10 percent, is admitted because of abuse on the part of caretakers. While abuse (an active intent on the part of the parent to injure or kill the child) is usually distinguished from the more passive process of neglect, severe neglect may in fact involve abuse. (See the later discussion on child abuse in the case of the Kelley family.) While 10 percent of the children may be admitted because of abuse, this does not mean that the incidence of abuse among children in foster care is only 10 percent. Estimates place the incidence much higher; perhaps as many as 40 percent of neglected and dependent children in care have been physically abused by their parents.

The final reason, accounting for about 30 percent of the cases (three in every ten children), is a global one called "other family problems." This is a catchall category covering a multitude of family problems, such as alcoholism, drug addiction, desertion, incompetence, arrest, foster home failure, and unwillingness of the parent to assume or continue care of the child.

These figures, like many social statistics, oversimplify what is a complex and multidetermined event. Seldom is there one clear-cut reason for admission. One thing does stand out, however: in only 15 percent of the cases are the child's own problems the reason for placement. In all the rest, it is the breakdown of the family unit (physical and mental illness of the parents) and the malfunctioning of the family (in abuse, neglect, and social problems) which necessitate the child's placement. Clearly what is involved is the inability of adults to care either for themselves or their children in a mature way.

The question that the child in foster care tries to understand, namely, "What happened to my parents that I had to leave them?" can best be answered by some illustrative cases. Each of the five cases to be presented has been chosen to illustrate one of the above reasons for placement. Each family is based on an actual case, but the accounts have been fictionalized to preserve confidentiality. Names, dates, places, family size, and so on have been altered. Each case is typical but not strictly biographical. The facts and events are real, in that none has been exaggerated or invented.

These cases show the varied impact on the child of the parents' inability to meet his needs adequately. They all involve child neglect, and the children themselves would fall under the general heading of "neglected and dependent" children.

CASE I – THE SOOLE FAMILY

A Case of Maternal Illness

Roger Soole had just turned three when his mother became pregnant. In the last month of her pregnancy, Mrs. Soole, twenty-eight, became depressed. She went to a private religious social service agency and asked if they could place Roger in a foster home for a month, as she needed bed rest and freedom from the responsibility of caring for him before her new baby was born. The agency, concerned about the mother's exhaustion and depression, placed Roger. They also discovered that the Soole family were having marital problems, but the mother refused any help, saying that all she needed was rest.

Roger stayed in the foster home for two months. He was miserable and unhappy at being separated from his mother. A month after the baby brother was born, at the agency's urging, Mrs. Soole took Roger back home. There was no further contact with the agency and the case was closed.

Almost exactly five years later, when Roger was eight, Mrs. Soole brought him to a child guidance clinic. She was crying, hysterical, and told a startled receptionist that she was afraid she would kill Roger. A clinic social worker saw the mother and found her extremely nervous, depressed, anxious, and very fearful of harming Roger. Mrs. Soole claimed the boy was impossible to manage and assaultive toward his younger brother.

The clinic took Mrs. Soole's fear of harming Roger seriously and that very day he was admitted to temporary emergency care in a child care institution. The clinic continued to work with the mother to try and clarify the situation. Gradually a story emerged of a mother who in the past few months had become increasingly nervous, depressed, irritable, erratic in her behavior, and a heavy drinker.

The case was referred to the state department of welfare, which took responsibility for it. A new, young worker assigned to the case judged the mother to be much less anxious and fearful of harming Roger than the clinic had reported, based on a home visit she made. (This probably was true, since much of the mother's anxiety and fear had been reduced by having Roger removed from the home.) Over the protests of the child care institution, she approved weekend visits home for Roger.

Roger visited home on weekends for a month. He returned to care each Sunday night with tales of brutal violence at home between his mother and father. Alarmed, the institution demanded that the state investigate the home situation. When a worker went to the home a week later, she found the mother had indeed been beaten by her husband.

Mr. Soole, thirty, had a history of violence as a juvenile. In junior high he had nearly killed another boy in a fistfight. Two years ago he had severely beaten a man in a tavern brawl. Though he never laid a hand (or fist) on the children, he did beat his wife regularly. The worker urged Mrs. Soole to take out a complaint against her husband, which she did. She immediately had a change of heart and warned her husband of what she had done. He promptly beat her again and then fled the state to avoid arrest. Roger's younger brother was taken into foster care and placed with a family at this time.

A few days later, Mrs. Soole showed up in the emergency ward of the city hospital, complaining of feeling sick, irritable, and depressed. In the course of the physical examination, she suddenly had a seizure. She was hospitalized and eventually a diagnosis was made of a brain tumor. (This apparently was unconnected with the beatings.) She was operated on and a sizable frontal tumor removed. She recovered well, surgically.

Unfortunately, so much brain matter was excised that

she had, in effect, been lobotomized. A marked change in her personality resulted. She became placid, irresponsible in her behavior, showed poor judgment, and lacked the ability to care for herself. She lived alone in a small apartment and was barely able to keep the house in decent condition.

Nonetheless, the state worker decided it would be good for the mother to have Roger at home with her on weekends, "to keep her mind off her other troubles." She also felt Roger was becoming institutionalized and should be with his mother. Over the protests of the institution, Roger went home for weekends. He returned each Sunday night deeply upset. He began bed-wetting, something he had not done before.

Still the visits went on until one weekend, Mrs. Soole, after drinking heavily, fell asleep in bed with a lighted cigarette in her hand.

The neighbors in the next apartment were awakened at three in the morning to find a hysterical Roger screaming that his mother was on fire. They rushed into the Soole apartment, found the bedroom in flames, dragged the unconscious and badly burned Mrs. Soole out, and called the fire department, the police, and an ambulance. Mrs. Soole, with burns over 60 percent of her body, was rushed to the hospital. Roger was returned kicking to the child care institution at five in the morning. For hours he kept screaming that his mother was dead. Finally he fell asleep.

Mrs. Soole did not die, although Roger has never seen her again. She spent months in painful recovery from her burns, which have left her badly crippled. There is no doubt now that she will never be able to care for Roger and his brother. Mr. Soole has completely disappeared from the picture. Roger and his brother have become two more orphans of the living.

COMMENTS ON THE SOOLE FAMILY

Not all cases of parental illness are as dramatic as that of the Soole family. Other cases involve chronic illnesses, heart defects, blindness, industrial accidents, auto accidents, ulcerative colitis, migraines, et cetera, but each has its own tragic aspects. Sometimes the illnesses are acute, and the parents recover. Almost always there is more involved than just illness. Frequently it is a poor marriage, to which the illness deals a final blow. If and when a family history is obtained, multiple problems are often uncovered, usually predating the illness said to be the reason for the placement. In Roger's case, there were indications of family breakdown at least five years earlier. Mother was having trouble with Roger and suffered from depression. She even placed him for two months in foster care and only reluctantly took him back after the baby was born.

That the family's management of angry feelings was a problem became clear when Roger was brought to a child guidance clinic because of his mother's fears that she would kill him. Sadly, she could not reveal at this time that she herself lived in fear of a brutal and assaultive husband. Roger was a witness to many acts of violence in his home.

Eventually Roger lost both parents: one through illness and accident, the other through desertion. Disturbances in his behavior appeared, such as bed-wetting, expressing the tensions in his life. Now, in care, he is fearful of violence, separation, and being deserted — all with adequate reason.

The last time Roger saw his mother she was engulfed in flames. When Roger grows up, what will be his most vivid memories of childhood?

CASE II — THE DOWNE FAMILY

A Psychotic Mother

Sally Downe was a pathetic, seven-year-old, blanket-wrapped bundle when she was carried into the child care center in the arms of a policeman. When he put her down, Sally, who had been asleep, woke up and screamed for her mother. The nurse tried to quiet her and found the child trembling all over. She was terribly frightened and with good reason. She had come very close to dying under the wheels of a subway train.

According to the policeman, Sally's mother had attempted suicide by climbing onto the tracks in a subway station and sitting down to wait for a train. Witnesses heard her saying that the state police were controlling her brain and forcing her to kill her child in order to save her from the sins of the world. A transit authority guard jumped into the pit to bring Sally and her mother to safety, but Mrs. Downe scrambled to her feet and held the child over the third rail. She threatened to drop the child if he came any closer. As the horrified crowd on the platform watched the tableau, they heard the distant rumble of a train.

Fortunately, another employee of the transit authority acted quickly to cut off the power to the third rail. He threw a block signal to red, and the approaching train screeched to a stop only feet from the mother and child. Realizing she wasn't going to die under the wheels of the train, Mrs. Downe threw herself and the child on the now dead third rail. When the guard reached her, both mother and child were screaming hysterically. Mrs. Downe was taken to a state hospital and Sally came into emergency care at a child care center while the police tried to locate her father.

It was three days before Mr. Downe finally showed up. When his wife and child had failed to return from shopping, he thought they had deserted him and he went on a weekend drunk. When he sobered up, he read the newspaper accounts of the incident at the train station and went to the police.

Mr. Downe was a thin, dull-appearing man who had only a sixth-grade education. He worked sporadically because of his drinking, at very unskilled and low-paying jobs. He revealed that his own father had died when he was five and he had been in a succession of foster homes until he was twenty-one years of age. He met and married his wife two years later. She had been working at the time as a waitress in a bar.

He could tell little about his wife except that she had been one of eight children. Her mother died when she was eleven and all the children had been placed in an orphanage. Mrs. Downe took it the hardest of all the children and became withdrawn from people. She had gone as far as the eighth grade in school and left the orphanage at eighteen.

He was vague about their early married life and couldn't remember Sally's birthdate. He did say his wife began acting strangely after Sally's birth, hearing voices and thinking that the people in the apartment above them were talking about her. On one occasion she had illegally placed Sally in a foster home for three months when she was two years old. When Sally was four, she had left her for a month with a neighbor. Recently she had gone downtown to Boston, stood on a street corner, and tried to give Sally away to passersby. He was unclear as to his wife's reason for doing this. When one of the people approached by the mother told a policeman about it, the police picked up Mrs. Downe and Sally and took them home. It was after that incident that Mrs. Downe began complaining that the state police were controlling her mind.

Mr. Downe said his wife tried to keep Sally a baby. She kept her on a bottle until she was five, at which time Mr. Downe threw it out. Sally was not toilet-trained and still in diapers (a fact that surprised the child care staff at the center when they undressed the child for bed that first night). Somehow Mrs. Downe had kept Sally home and never sent her to school.

Subsequent information from the state hospital where Mrs. Downe was confined revealed her to be agitated, suspicious, hostile, argumentative, hallucinating, and delusional. She was diagnosed as a paranoid schizophrenic. Later information showed she had been hospitalized five previous times with the same diagnosis for brief periods, a fact Mr. Downe neglected to mention during his interview.

Sally remained in placement at the child care center because her father felt unable to care for her without his wife. Sally turned out to be a chronic bed wetter and withheld feces as well. She was hospitalized twice during the follow-

ing months for fecal impaction. Sally remained in an institution for neglected children for two years and then was
sent to a small group home. Three years later, she was still
there. Her mother was in a mental hospital again and her
father was living with another woman. He had no desire
to have Sally with him and he never visited her. The group
home where Sally had been placed was over a hundred miles
from where Mr. Downe lived and he gave the distance as
an excuse for not visiting.

COMMENTS ON THE DOWNE FAMILY
The marriage of two chronically inadequate people quite
predictably results in an inadequate family. Both Mr. and
Mrs. Downe were barely able to meet their own needs,
much less those of a spouse and a child. The situation is
made even worse when one parent is psychotic. All neglected children show deviation in their behavior and development, but the child of a psychotic parent pays an especially
terrible price in growing up. (Generally it is true that the
more severe the pathology of the home, the more disturbed
is the child's behavior.)

Children need so many things in order to develop into
physically and emotionally healthy adults. Most easily met
are their physical needs, for food, clothing, and shelter. But
they also need medical care when they are ill and, ideally,
extensive preventive medical care.

Less easily seen by most people are the child's emotional
needs. Babies don't simply need to be loved. The quality
of that love is so very important. It needs to be consistent,
constant care by the same person (not necessarily the biological mother). Children need to be stimulated by people
(through talking, rocking, cuddling, bathing, feeding, and
so on) and also by things (sounds, colors, smells, feels, and
tastes). They need toys appropriate to their age to manipulate and the freedom to explore their world. From all these
things and many more, the child learns socially, to respond
to people, to trust them, to laugh, to enjoy, to feel good

about himself and the kind of world he lives in, and to want to do things, such as learn, grow, share, work, play, and satisfy others.

The source of most of this early learning so important to the child's eventual healthy development is the family. From them he learns that he is cared for and worthwhile, that he is competent and pleasing to others.

Parents have so much to do to raise a child, but what they do is not nearly so important as what they are. They must be mature enough to be able to meet a child's needs: comfort him when he is sick; support him when he is discouraged; encourage him to try to do his best; and most importantly, to serve as a model to the child for the kind of person he can become.

When children don't get these things, they show deviations in their development. Sometimes they don't grow physically or mentally, but most often they fail to develop emotionally and socially. There are many deviations in behavior common among children who are neglected. Some are developmental disorders, like disturbance in motility (such as hyperactivity, head-banging, or excessive rocking in the crib). Many don't show the normal crying response of young children separated from their mothers. Others exhibit sleeping or eating disturbances, such as pica, in which the young child eats inedible things like dirt, stones, or plaster. Some neglected children are apathetic or unresponsive and don't smile easily; others are irritable and fret constantly. Some avoid relationships with people, while others will run to rub up against any adult, even complete strangers, seeking the affection and close body contact they never received enough of when small.

Almost invariably, children with developmental disturbances are found to have seriously disturbed relationships with their mothers, often because the mother is psychotic or near-psychotic. Psychosis may disrupt the mother's ability to plan for the child, to keep the house in order, or even to see the child as a separate person. Often these mothers themselves have had severe traumas in their own childhood and poor mothering, and they identify with their own babies in these terms. Mrs. Downe lost her mother through death and was brought up in an orphanage. To make up for her own loss, she wanted Sally to have a happy babyhood. Her need for Sally to be a baby extended far beyond Sally's normal babyhood. Mrs. Downe infantilized her child by keeping her in diapers and on a bottle until the father threw the bottle out when Sally was five years old. She also kept Sally out of school so that the two of them could be together.

Mr. Downe was unable to help his wife let Sally grow up. Sally paid the price for Mrs. Downe's distorted needs for a baby by developing somatic symptoms, bed-wetting and withholding feces. Part of her still remained mother's baby, needing to be changed and toileted by a mother. Part of Sally never grew up, and indeed, may never grow up.

A psychotic mother communicates with her child in psychotic ways, and if the child is ever to have its needs met, it has to learn these distorted ways of reaching the mother. If this goes on for too long without intervention, the child may never be able to give up the distorted ways it has learned to communicate with others. Then someday she too may become a mother and will teach her child how to be psychotic. Sally's persisting symptoms while in care were nonverbal cries for her mother to come and care for her. They were inappropriate and aroused anger and disgust in many adults who cared for her. The one for whom she cried didn't come and the ones who came instead didn't hear her cry.

CASE III – THE MYERS FAMILY

A Problem Child in a Problem Family

Phillip, at the age of eight and a half, was placed in institutional care voluntarily by his mother, in order to "find out what is wrong with him." Mrs. Myers could no longer tolerate Phillip at home. He was overly active, would not mind her, and sadistically taunted his younger sisters, keeping the house in turmoil. Mrs. Myers expressed concern that Phillip, the second oldest of her four children, would get into some kind of trouble and turn out to be just like his father, a man whom she had divorced some years before because he was abusive to the children and to her.

In her late thirties, Mrs. Myers was the product of an exceedingly unhappy childhood. By five years of age she had already been physically abused by her parents and there was some suspicion that she had been sexually molested by her father. When she was six, her parents were divorced and Mrs. Myers was placed in a foster home. Her mother immediately married again and moved out-of-state, leaving her daughter behind. It was five years before the state located her and forced her to take back her child. There followed more years of neglect for Mrs. Myers and constant exposure to her mother's sexual misbehavior.

When Mrs. Myers was in her early teens, her mother's extramarital activities resulted in a pregnancy. When the husband (Mrs. Myers's stepfather) saw that the baby was obviously not Caucasian, he divorced his wife. He wanted to take his stepdaughter to live with him, but circumstances prevented this, so Mrs. Myers was once again placed in a foster home.

She spent the next five years in a succession of foster homes to which she adjusted poorly. She remembers these homes bitterly as places where "they got all the work they could out of you and never gave you any love in return." Agency records contain the comments of some of the foster parents that Mrs. Myers was "irresponsible, lacked integrity and engaged in repeated sexual escapades."

Shortly after leaving foster care, in her early twenties, Mrs. Myers became pregnant out of wedlock. She kept the child and two years later married another man who fathered Phillip. Shortly after the boy's birth, she divorced her husband because of his abusiveness to the children and to her.

A few years later she was pregnant again. This time, just like her mother, she produced a child of mixed race. A few years later, it was another mixed-racial child with a different father. Six months after the birth of this child, she asked for placement for Phillip.

A year and a half later, Phillip was still in placement at the same institution. Mrs. Myers continued to live on welfare with her remaining three children. She no longer received an allotment for Phillip, since he was out of the home. She rarely visited him and made no plans for his eventual return to her. As she put it to her last caseworker, "Why should I take him back? The extra money I'd get from welfare wouldn't be worth all the trouble he'd give me." Evidently the state agreed, for Mrs. Myers no longer has a family worker assigned to her.

COMMENT ON THE MYERS FAMILY

The Myers family is typical of many of the families of children who come into foster care. One of the first things the case illustrates is how very difficult it is to point to any one reason for a child coming into care. The Myers case is given as an example of the problems of a child leading to placement. There is obviously considerable social pathology present in this family. This is a one-parent family, on welfare, with a number of illegitimate children in the family. The mother is inadequate to the task of raising any of the children. One could ask why Phillip was placed while the state allowed the others to remain at home? Was there something unique about the family's pathology, the mother's problems, and the character of this particular child which interacted to make him unacceptable to the mother? She sees Phillip as the focus of her troubles, raising the question, "What is wrong with him?" Obviously she has problems, too, and they span a generation and possibly more if we had an adequate history of the grandparents.

A second point is that the parents of neglected and dependent children who are in foster care were often children in foster care themselves. Deprived children have parents who were deprived by their parents in childhood. In some cases this chain of cause and effect can be traced

back through three or four generations. Clearly society has
been providing the illusion of caring for some time and
their interventions have not been effective in breaking the
chain of deprivation. In short, public neglect has become
a substitute for private neglect.

A third factor apparent in all these cases is the overwhelming amount of family and social pathology. There
are families broken by mental and physical illness, divorce
and separation, frequent one-parent families (six million
children in this country live with only a mother as a parent),[4]
and the almost inevitable poverty (75 percent of the families
headed by a woman have an income under $6,000 a year).[5]
Social pathology is apparent in sexual acting out, adultery,
illegitimate children, incest, and the high frequency of
people on welfare.

A fourth point to keep in mind is the compulsive need
of children to recreate their parents' past life history. Some
consider this an example of children's identification with
their parents. In Mrs. Myers's case, her identification with
the model of her mother as a woman led to frequent sexual
acting out, adultery, illegitimate children, impregnation by
a member of another race, marrying an abusive man, divorce,
and the placing of a child in foster care. Not only that,
but Mrs. Myers is hard at work seeing to it that another
generation repeat the sins of their fathers, by constantly
degrading Phillip's father in front of him and directly expressing concern that Phillip is going to grow up to be "just
like his father." In all likelihood, Phillip is well on his way
to becoming an adult male who will father a child out of
wedlock, perhaps marry the girl, end up abusing her and
the children, being divorced, and leaving it up to society
to care for another generation of foster children.

The Myers case history demonstrates the tendency of
parents of children in care to repeat the life-styles of their
own parents. Later on, in focusing on the children in care,
it will be seen how they need to reproduce their traumatic
homelife in their relationships with the adults who take

care of them. The child's identification with the negative images set by inadequate parents is a source of social infection as real as that of contagious physical illnesses, such as measles, chicken pox, and VD. Simply removing the child from the home by no means prevents the spread of this social infection, for the germs lie breeding in the minds of the children. Unless the infection is treated, it will someday erupt into view.

Another point to consider in this case is the lack of any plan for Phillip. No one is working with the mother; she is not eager to have Phillip returned to her care. By default he has remained in foster care for a year and a half. For two-thirds to three-quarters of the children in foster care, this is the reality of their existence. There is no plan as to whether and under what circumstances they can return home.

Children who remain in care for longer than a year and a half become a high risk group. The chances are very great that they will remain in foster care indefinitely, truly children in limbo. The longer a child stays in foster care, the more likely he is to show signs of severe emotional disturbance.

One final point about the Myers family. Poverty alone is not the cause of their problems. Money alone will not solve their problems. Even with higher welfare grants, Phillip probably would have come into care. Contraceptive and/or abortion services could have been provided, but it is unlikely that Mrs. Myers would have availed herself of them. An agency note expresses the opinion that "Mrs. Myers needs psychologically to have a baby to love and be dependent on her. She will continue to have illegitimate children. Since her focus is on babies, this is the only way she knows of loving and caring for her children. It is predicted that her relationship with her children will become poorer as they grow older."

What these children and their parents need, more than anything else, is someone who cares.

CASE IV – THE KELLEY FAMILY

A Child Is Beaten

The original contact with the Kelley family came about as the result of an anonymous phone call to the Society for the Prevention of Cruelty to Children, reporting that the Kelley children were being abused and left unattended for long periods of time. When a worker visited the home to investigate, she was admitted by a six-year-old who reported that his parents were not at home. The worker found five children, ages eight, six, four, and three years, and fifteen months, left in the care of the oldest child.

The Kelley apartment was a shambles, cluttered with junk and a suspiciously large number of small appliances still in their original cartons, probably stolen merchandise. The children were dressed in their pajamas even though it was three o'clock in the afternoon and the baby was crying in his crib in a darkened room. He was obviously hungry and needed to be changed. The bedclothes, the walls near the child, and the child himself were smeared with feces. All of the children complained of not having eaten since the night before.

The worker checked the kitchen and found the refrigerator empty except for three bottles of beer. The stench from a pile of thoroughly rotting garbage in the kitchen caused her to retch. Animal feces, from one or more dogs, lay in piles on the kitchen floor. The three-year-old complained of feeling sick and when the worker felt her forehead, the child was quite warm. (She was subsequently found to have a temperature of 103 degrees.) The four-year-old had a black eye, bruises on the upper extremities, and what looked like cigarette burns on her legs.

A Care and Protection petition was taken out against the parents and the children were removed from their home and placed in a foster home. Within three months, the new foster mother complained of the four-year-old's behavior. The child, a girl with the improbable first name of Kelly, was said to be hyperactive, enuretic, given to smearing feces on the bedroom walls, broke all her toys, and "talked funny." The foster mother also complained that the oldest children were destructive and unmanageable. The two oldest children were placed in a child care institution while Kelly and her two younger siblings were transferred to another foster home which the state welfare worker thought might be more tolerant of their behavior.

Four months later, the welfare worker visited the Kelley children in their new foster home for the first time since she had placed them there. She was shocked to find the children were being mistreated and severely neglected. They were apathetic, had lost weight, and were covered with bruises. She immediately removed the children from the home and placed them with their other siblings in the child care center. The state took away the foster home's license and closed it down.

The children's parents had made no objection to their removal into foster home care. The children's mother, Mrs. Kelley, age thirty, had a history of delinquent behavior and sexual promiscuity as a child. By the time she was twenty-two, she had been married, divorced, placed an illegitimate child for adoption, been in jail for six months and in a mental hospital for three months. After her discharge from the state hospital, she began drinking heavily. Within six months, she married Mr. Kelley, whom she had met in a bar.

Mr. Kelley, age thirty-five, had been a foster child since age four, when his mother died and his father deserted. He was unmanageable in the home and spent the years from age eight to sixteen in a reform school. At the time of his marriage, he had an extensive criminal record. When the Care and Protection petition was taken out, a routine check of court and probation records turned up a history of thirty-seven arrests (assault and battery, four; drunk and disorderly, fifteen; breaking and entering, two; lewd and lascivious behavior, three; and thirteen counts of vagrancy). He was an abusive man when drunk, given to violent beatings of both his wife and children. He had once tied his wife to a kitchen chair and systematically punched out ten of her teeth.

The Kelley children remained in care for two years and then a new state welfare worker took over the case and decided to return the children to the parents. There was no evidence that the parents had changed their life-style in any way — in fact, they had refused to accept help from the social worker and had never visited the children while they were in care. The week before the children were scheduled to return home, Mr. Kelley got drunk and severely beat his wife, causing her to miscarry her seventh child. The next day he was arrested on a charge of armed robbery after an attempted holdup of a liquor store. He was subsequently convicted and sentenced to a lengthy term in state prison.

The Kelley children also continue to serve their time in a different kind of prison. They do not know where their father is, never see their mother, and no longer even have a caseworker assigned to them by the state. (Caseworkers are scarce, they are assigned more cases than they can humanly handle, and priorities are given to cases that show some possibility for rehabilitation.)

Meanwhile, the Kelley children are in limbo, six more children serving an indefinite sentence for the crime of choosing their parents unwisely.

COMMENTS ON THE KELLEY FAMILY

The Kelley family raises the specter of child abuse. In contrast to neglect, which is usually a passive process, child abuse involves the parents' or other caretakers' active, usually deliberate intent to cause physical injury to the child. Child abuse is not a common social problem in the United States, but it is a serious one. It is serious when the Joint Commission on the Mental Health of Children reports that the nationwide total of child abuse cases is two to three thousand a month, with one or two children killed each day in the United States by parents. One medical source, quoted by the Commission, reports that the number of children under five who are killed by parents each year is higher than the number of those who die from disease.[6]

The true incidence of child abuse in the population is extremely difficult to discover. The reasons have to do with the lack of an adequate working definition of child abuse, problems of differential diagnosis, and bias in samples used to generate statistics on child abuse.

If a very broad definition is used, for example, the use of physical force by a caretaker toward a child, in order to hurt, injure, or destroy the child,[7] and if we had a way of knowing when each such use of force occurred, the incidence of child abuse would run into millions of cases each year. If a narrow definition is used, based on the extent of injury involved, and restricted to the serious injury end of the spectrum, then Gil [8] reports that of six to seven thousand official reports a year of child abuse, over half of these were minor injuries and the classical battered child was rather rare. Another source, reporting a study of 662 abused children, showed more than half were under four years of age and that approximately 25 percent of those (mostly infants age two or younger) died as a result.[9]

Another difficulty is the problem in differential diagnosis between child abuse and childhood accidents. Parents of battered children almost invariably present their children as accident victims when seeking medical care. Even in some legitimate accidents, there may be a factor of parental neglect or lack of supervision that stems from an unconscious hostility toward the child by the parent. (Example: the child of two who was left on a bed next to an open second-story window which he eventually fell out of. The mother reported she had meant to close the window but had "forgotten" to do so.)

Pediatric roentgenology has helped in the differential diagnostic problem by pointing out the association of multiple fractures of the long bones and subdural hematomas in young abused children, but the problem is still a difficult one to decide. Add to this the hesitation of some medical personnel to confront parents with their suspicions that the child has been abused, and until recently, the threat of being sued if the accusation was false, and the problem is compounded.

Every state and territory in the United States now has child abuse reporting laws, but these exert more influence on the doctor working in a hospital than on the physician in private practice. The less intense the doctor-patient relationship, the easier it is to report the patient. The laws, of course, are in opposition to the legally protected doctor-patient relationship in some states and the universally held "ethical" commitment of the doctor to protect his patients' confidential communications.[10]

The problem of statistical bias is hard to get around, but one can at least be aware of its existence. Many studies on the incidence of child abuse have been hospital studies. The bias here is probably toward the younger child, since he is easier to injure and more likely to be injured severely, necessitating hospitalization. If the study is done in the emergency ward of a hospital, further bias is introduced through the nature of those who use this service. It is frequently used by the poor, who use the emergency ward instead of a private pediatrician or general physician.

Incidence studies that rely on formal cases reported through legal channels or newspaper accounts of child abuse are also likely to err toward overrepresenting the poor. Gil's study at Brandeis University, done for the Children's Bureau,[11] surveyed cases reported through legal channels during 1967–1968 and uncovered thirteen thousand incidents. Estimates of the number of undetected cases that are never reported could easily double that figure. The Child Welfare League of America estimates ten thousand cases per year of child brutality.[12]

It is surprising that child abuse incidence figures are not greater. Two cultural factors predispose child abuse as an endemic problem in our society. Our definition of child-rearing practices does not clearly exclude the use of physical force toward children. Corporal punishment is still sanctioned in our institutions that deal with children (schools, reformatories, child care institutions, and so on). A 1969 National Educational Association poll found that 65 percent of elementary school teachers favored the judicious use of physical punishment in the classroom.[13] Only in the last few years was the use of the rattan outlawed in the Boston schools. This step was taken over the howling protests of some teachers who claimed they were being divested of their last means of discipline over the children. Howard James,[14] in his study of the treatment of juvenile delinquents in the United States, reports examples of brutality against child inmates of these institutions, in the name of correction and discipline. The law in most jurisdictions is unable to draw the line where the use of force for "discipline" crosses over into brutality. Unless the parent inflicts permanent injury or acts with extreme cruelty and malice, society tends not to interfere with the parent's right to discipline his child. One mother, overheard in a psychiatric clinic waiting room, commented on the behavior of an abusive mother, "If she wants to beat her kid, she can beat him. It's her business, not mine." [15] Another mother, responding to the suggestion that her children be placed, screamed at the worker, "I want to beat them myself. Nobody else is allowed to beat them but me." [16] At least she knew her rights as a parent.

Let one adult touch another without his consent and technically assault and battery have been committed. But a parent can beat up a child in the name of discipline and few will interfere, as long as he doesn't break bones or cause blood to flow.[17] This points up a second cultural factor in child abuse, namely, that our old English tradition of common law accepts the parent's right to punish and discipline children, because we essentially still see children as the property of their parents and not as human beings in their own right. Children have very few, if any, legal rights and those they do have are often subordinated to parental rights.

Many of our traditional ways of handling child welfare problems have grown out of English common law. Not only are they archaic when applied to modern times, but they are frequently in opposition to the welfare of the child. The legal and cultural question in child welfare for the future is going to be, "Is American society going to make a basic commitment to the welfare of children by spelling out equivalent rights for children as now held by adults and then backing those rights with legislation and funds?"

The Abusing Family

There are a number of danger signs in family life that make child abuse likely, though we do very little to help relieve these strains. Poverty, marital conflict, social isolation, and the overwhelmed mother are four of these signs. These factors describe about 90 percent of abusing families.

Abusing parents tend to be young and emotionally immature people. There is a high rate of bio-psycho-social deviance among these parents as well as considerable deviance in family structure. Among abusing families there is a high proportion of female-headed households (30 percent in one study) [18] where the biological father is absent. More mothers than fathers abuse children, probably because the latter aren't around much, if at all, and don't share in the strains of caring for children. Usually there are more children in such families than in the average American family (more strain on mother). The incidence of serious injuries in child abuse tend to be concentrated among the poor, nonwhite population (remember statistical bias).

Abusing adults often delay seeking medical care for their child, in spite of the obvious seriousness of the injuries. Often they present the child to the doctor as an "accident" victim. The evasion and contradictions in the parent's story of how the child was injured are often tip-offs to battering. The histories as presented just don't agree with the clinical findings. Multiple skeletal injuries, multiple soft-tissue injuries, signs of injuries in various stages of healing, and the correlation between subdural hematoma and long bone injuries are some of the medical signs that point to battering.

The abusing adult tends to shop around for medical treatment. If hospitals and doctors could pool their information, they would find the incident of child abuse they are dealing with probably was not the first one. Those who abuse children tend to be involved in multiple incidents. The abused child frequently has abused siblings at home. In fairness to the abusing parent, the likelihood is great that as a child he too was abused and beaten by his parents. A poignant reminder of that was the battered child in institutional care who was overheard playing with her doll. She was beating it with a stick and saying, "Bad dolly for doing that. Now I am going to beat you until you are black and blue." Someday she'll be a real mother and the doll will be a flesh-and-blood baby, and she will care for him in the only way she knows how to love, by beating him black and blue.

Frequently, abusing parents have been deprived of nurturance, emotional warmth, and parental concern as children. They become deeply disturbed and violent adults. They grow up yearning for a loving mother and with a fury against the world for depriving them of such a mother. Often there is a role reversal in which the abusing parents seek nurturance and care from their children (which is part of what is meant by emotionally immature). When the children don't give, but demand instead, they become a target for parental anger. (Lower-class mothers tend to punish children for excessive demands, crying, and disobedience; middle- and upper-class mothers punish aggressive activity.)

Sometimes this parental anger is actually projected onto the children, who are seen as mean or hostile to the parent. One such mother swore that she could look into her baby's eyes and see his hatred of her. "He's mean to me and hates me," she said, "just like everyone else." Another was terrified of her baby and screamed, "If he comes home, he'll be up in the cemetery with the other one, the one I liked. I'm so scared I can't touch him. I shove the bottle at him. He looks at me as if he hates me. I've barely touched him since the other one died." [19]

The anger toward the child, sometimes identified as a hated figure of the parent's own childhood (the bad mother, or hated sibling or relative), is not always verbally expressed. It doesn't matter because it hurts the child either way, as in the case of the mother who gave a boiling water enema to her one-year-old child.

Frequently, abusing parents use violent language, as the mother who called her child to dinner with, "Get in this house before I knock your block off." Anger over deprivation lies at the base of the abusing parent. One parent, faced with placement of her children, threatened, "I'll kill them before they take them from me."

These parents cannot parent because they were not parented. They cannot give to their children because they have nothing to give and need being cared for so much. As children, they too had only the illusion of caring.

As one might expect, abusing families often rely on physical means of control of their children, such as spanking and whipping. In parental rages, this often gets out of control and real damage is done. The two-hundred-pound father who worked over his twenty-pound daughter until her skull split, said, "I goofed beating the kid on the skull. I've always beaten her where it didn't show." [20]

The parents' inability to see the child as a unique individual and not like some hated figure from their past leads to distortions and failure to understand the child's needs. For example, many abusing mothers saw small infants as needing discipline, because they could "consciously" misbehave. In one study, such mothers believed babies should know right from wrong by twelve months and one-third of the mothers put this figure at six months.[21] In the same study, 80 percent of abusive mothers said they would hit back against infant aggression in order to show the child that he is not to do that sort of thing. (The incidence of this behavior in nonabusive, but also largely lower-class mothers, was 63 percent.) Hitting a child doesn't teach him not to hit others; it only teaches him that it is all right for big people to beat up little people and that he should

"What makes me angry is when my father puts my head in the toilet"
— *six-year-old boy*

wait until he is grown up and then he too can beat up his children.

The Abused Children

There may be fewer young abused children than we used to think, but it is clear that these are the ones most likely to be seriously injured. More boys than girls tend to be abused, except among teen-agers, where the reverse is true. (Incest is a form of child abuse, too.)

On the average, the second child tends to be the abused one. This probably goes along with the finding that the birth of a sibling either one year before or nine months after the incidence of abuse is an important factor. Mothers are under more strain when pregnant or when dealing with more than one small child. If they are really overwhelmed when dealing with one child, something is going to let loose when they have more than one.

It is not surprising to find that abused children, if they escape serious physical damage (crippling, brain damage, and retardation are possible), have serious psychological damage. They have marked difficulty with impulse control and the management of their anger. They are often hostile toward the world generally and other adults specifically. They have poor self-concepts. (Why else should they have been beaten, than because they were bad and not capable of being loved by anyone?) They grow up to become parents who beat their own children, even as they were beaten.

It is difficult for many people to accept the fact that there are parents who can and do kill their children. Or if they reluctantly admit their existence, these parents are dismissed as "obviously crazy." Even more dangerous is the assumption that parents who beat their children either didn't mean to do it or didn't know any better. Once the case of an abused child comes to the attention of the law, too many naïve judges, social workers, or other authorities believe that surely now these parents have learned their lesson and, if they are given another chance, they will realize and accept their responsibilities as parents and stop beating their children.

This is extremely dangerous wishful thinking. Experience shows that all too often, if a battered baby is returned to his parents and no help is given to the parents, the result is renewed beatings. Tragically, the next beating is usually the fatal one. Stern lectures and threats of legal sanctions to the parents do little to control impulses and are no substitute for psychiatric help; they are more likely a signed death certificate for the child.

CASE V – THE HANSEN FAMILY

The Family That Wasn't

The Hansens were never a family in the social sense.[22] Mrs. Hansen had been placed in a state school for the retarded by her family when she was three years old. At that time, she was estimated to have had an IQ of 50. She lived in the school until she was nineteen, having little or no contact with her family. Then one fine spring weekend, she ran away to find her parents. She was found two weeks later in a flophouse in Boston, hungry, disheveled, but apparently unhurt. It was two months later before the staff at the state school discovered Mrs. Hansen was pregnant. She did not know who the father was.

The child, Mark, was born seven months later at the school's infirmary. His mother was intellectually incapable of caring for him, and the infirmary staff raised Mark for the first year and a half of his life. No attempt had been made to place him for adoption because the staff suspected that Mark, too, was retarded. Whether this was inherited retardation or the effects of the sterile environment of the school's infirmary, or both, was hard to say. Some of the staff thought the child might do better if placed in a foster home. A foster home for a retarded child is not easy to find, but the school did it, and Mark went to live with an elderly couple when he was two years old.

He lived with them for ten years and, during that time, his IQ steadily climbed from 50 (as measured at two when he was placed) to the low 80's. Mark attended public school and managed to get promoted each year. It is not clear from the record why Mark wasn't adopted by this family, but his long "temporary" stay ended when he was twelve years old. The foster mother died suddenly and the foster father felt he was unable to keep Mark and requested his removal from the home. Mark's IQ was now in the low 90's, too high to allow him back in the school for the retarded, so he was placed instead in a child care institution for the neglected and dependent child. (Foster homes for adolescent boys are even harder to find.)

Mark has been in the institution for three years now. The plans for his future are very indefinite. He is too old to stay at the institution any longer. He has to leave, but there is no place for him to go. He has no home, family, or known relatives — yet he is not an orphan. He is too young to be on his own. Small group homes, residential high schools, or treatment centers for disturbed adolescents are both expensive and hard to find. There are too few places and too many who need help.

Mark needs a supervised setting and psychiatric help. He is a lonely, confused boy with no clear self-image and deep feelings of rejection and not belonging to anyone. He is obsessed with finding out about his past history and locating his missing father and mother. (His mother was discharged from the hospital ten years ago, unknown to the state welfare department and has disappeared.) No matter who cares for him or how well, Mark is chronically unhappy about how he is treated. He wants what he cannot have, to belong to a mother and a father who love him. He has what he does not want, an institution of strangers who care for him. He is forever searching for what he lost as an infant. As Mark said in a poem he wrote: "Loneliness is missing somebody who never said good-bye."

Once, in looking at the thin beige folder that is all that is known about him and his early life, Mark blurted out, "I'm not a real person. My life is just a summary." He flung the record on the floor and burst into tears.

COMMENTS ON THE HANSEN FAMILY

Very few people would expect that Mrs. Hansen would be able to care for Mark. A woman with an IQ of 50, who is in institutional care herself, can't understand the complexities of being an adult, much less a parent. In her way, too, Mrs. Hansen is a child. She is intellectually and emotionally immature, needing much the same kind of care that Mark does.

It is equally true that all of the neglecting parents in this book are retarded in some way. Most of them are not severely intellectually retarded like Mrs. Hansen, although some of them may be of dull normal intelligence. They are all, however, emotionally retarded. In varying degrees, in one or more areas of their emotional lives, they have failed to grow and develop adequately.

The five cases presented here have illustrated the "reasons" for children coming into placement. Marital conflicts, physical and mental illnesses, the normal demands of children, alcoholism, drug addiction, the unusual demands of problem children, retardation — these things are all stresses on the parent which he or she is unable to cope with successfully. Indeed, some of these stresses are also symptoms (for example, alcoholism, marital conflicts, mental illness) of the same emotional immaturity that leads to child neglect.

These parents are not emotionally immature because they neglect their children; rather they neglect their children because they are emotionally immature. Neglecting parents are seeking the very same things their children are seeking, namely love, security, nurturance, increased self-esteem, and so on. In addition, they seek these things in ways appropriate to a child and not to an adult. They are, in effect, not parents to their children but often rivals of them for the world's limited supply of love. They make poor parents because they place the satisfaction of their own needs first, and those of their children a distant second.

Not that healthy parents always put their children's needs before their own. That is masochistic martyrdom in the grand American tradition and scarcely healthy for children or parents. Nor is it to say that healthy adults don't need love, security, increased self-esteem, and so on, because they do. But healthy adults don't feel so emotionally crippled, unloved, and inadequate to obtain these things that they have to compete with their children to get them. Mature adults get satisfaction of their needs through social contacts with other adults, in the intimacy of marriage, in productive work, and in the loving care of their children. They do these things and are able to give love as well as take it, to be reasonably successful and happy and feel good about themselves, while the neglecting parent is inadequate to do these things, can only take love, is selfish and narcissistic, and spends his time in the fruitless pursuit of satisfying his own needs and has neither time nor energy left over to care for anyone else.

The reason healthy adults can be good parents is simple: they had good parents. As children, their emotional needs were met adequately by their parents, and they were able to grow and develop. Without exception, it is found that neglecting parents were not adequately parented when they were children; their emotional needs were not satisfied. Emotionally deprived children grow up to be emotionally deprived adults. When they become parents, they do not know how to parent their own children adequately. Then, under some circumstances, the children may have to be removed from the home.

The removal of a child from his parents is difficult on everyone involved, parent, child, and social worker. Often inexperienced workers are confused by the obvious neglect, on the one hand, and the parents' expressions of love for their child and their desire to keep him. The worker hesitates, believing that feelings and actions must be related, so that a parent who loves his child will care for him or that a parent who wants to keep his child will care for him, so you shouldn't take the child away.

The issue is not whether the parents say they love the child or not; it is whether they are able to care for the child. Can the parents translate expressions of love into appropriate care that meets the child's needs? It is the inability of neglecting parents to do this that results in the neglect of the child.

On the day the child is placed, many parents report feelings of sadness, or of worry and nervousness. Some report no feeling at all, which is usually indicative of the inability to deal with the feelings involved. Interestingly enough, how parents feel is related to the reason for the child's placement. Thankfulness was common in parents whose children had been placed because of the mother's physical illness. Guilt and relief were common among the parents when behavior problems of the child were the reason for placement. Anger, on the other hand, is most common in cases where parental abuse and family dysfunction are the reasons for placement.[23]

Other studies of parents whose children are in foster care show that these parents tend to view the world from a calculating and hostile point of view. Many of them feel socially alienated. The more they feel alienated, the more frequent was anger a placement reaction. (Those whose orientation toward society was more trusting more often felt shame.) The parents of the abused child most often felt that the social agency which placed their child was a usurper of parental rights rather than a surrogate acting *in loco parentis.*

Another interesting finding is that two-thirds of the parents in the sample of one study had strongly authoritarian child-rearing attitudes. Strong authoritarian attitudes are often related to emotional immaturity.

One alcoholic mother commented on her child's placement, "I was sad, I was hurt, I cried all the way home. Now I knew I would be alone." Here one clearly sees that the parent's thoughts and feelings are of herself. There is no worry or concern expressed about how the child is doing without her or how the child must be feeling. Another mother said, "It felt like death," which is how children see separation. A father whose child had been placed experienced it in terms of reliving his own childhood. "It made me think back to the time I was placed [in foster care]. I felt funny inside, like I was alone again." [24] One aspect of emotional immaturity is the ease with which present adult experiences evoke unmodulated childhood feelings.

One final point can be made about these cases. In spite of ringing testimonials to the value and integrity of family life, our commitment is not much more than hollow words. Too often, in times of family crises, the public response is to split up the family. We are not committed in practice and do little to implement the preservation of family ties. Sometimes having no other choice, families must allow their children to be placed, for there is a dearth of homemaker services, day care centers for working parents, family counseling aid, and — perhaps the biggest lack of all

— any form of public education or training for the job of raising children and being a family. For so much of life there seems to be no adequate education.

To child and parent alike, placement means the loss of an emotionally important person. The placed child loses his most important supports, his parents. It makes no difference how inadequate those parents may have been; they were the child's only parents and emotionally important to him. Once you break up a family, it is rather like Humpty Dumpty; no one can put it back together again. A child should be placed in foster care only after every available resource to hold the family together has been exhausted.

No matter how inadequate the care the child was receiving, from his point of view, when he is placed, it is even worse, because then he has nothing. His next concern is then, "Who will take care of me?" The Appendix tries to provide one answer to that question by reviewing the history of child care practices for neglected and dependent children in the United States.

"What makes me really mad is when my mother and father put me out in the cold. Then they put me on a chain like a dog."
— seven-year-old boy

2

Why Am I Here?

"The only reason that I can think of for my mother not to want me is if there is something terribly wrong with me or something terribly wrong with her. Either way, I've had it."

"I figure that I must have done something pretty bad for my mother not to want me. I was only ten days old when my mother got rid of me. The only thing that I can think of that a ten-day-old baby could do wrong was to cry a lot. I've thought back as far as I can, and I don't remember crying that much."

— CHILDREN IN FOSTER CARE

It would seem that the question a child in placement asks — namely, "Why am I here?" — has already been answered in Chapter 1. He is told again and again by substitute caretakers, "You are here because your parents have problems and are unable to take care of you properly."

But these adults speak to the child with the voice of reality about objective reasons for his separation from his parents. For the child, reality is subjective; it is how he feels about what has happened to him that counts. Children who are separated from their parents, no matter what the reason for that separation, experience it as a loss. They feel abandoned, rejected, anxious and afraid, and often empty, worthless, humiliated, unimportant, and helpless. Their helplessness is obvious in their complete lack of control over the parents leaving them.

These feelings are not unique to the child in foster care. They are common to all children separated from their parents, but greatly intensified in the placed child. A child's sense of security and stability grows out of his relationship with his parents. He is so helpless and dependent upon them for care and protection that he cannot imagine ever being able to live without them. When our entire well-being depends so much on someone whom we need, it is only human to worry about losing that person. Thus, a natural but deeply buried fear of every child is that he will lose his parents.

Of course, every child does leave his parents, little by little, day by day. Separations of parent and child do occur, inevitably. The parents go out for an evening, leaving the child at home or perhaps they take a vacation together, leaving the child with grandmother. Parents and children do get sick and have to be hospitalized. Sometimes parents die when children are young. Or maybe the separation is psychological, such as having to share your parents with a newborn sibling. Whatever the reason, whenever separations occur, children feel threatened, rejected, and abandoned. The normal, healthy child survives these separations, gradually learns to master the feelings aroused by separation, and grows stronger knowing he has endured, mastered, and survived. He grows to need his parents less because he has their emotional support most of the time.

When a child is placed in foster care, the fear of losing his parents becomes a shattering reality. He does not know when, or if, he will ever be reunited with them again. The impact of this event on the child is overwhelming and he cannot begin to handle the intense feelings of terror, sadness, and loss aroused. Perhaps most destructive of all to the child's future mental health is failure to come to grips with the intense anger that separation arouses. Typical of how the child feels are these comments by placed children.

"I was so scared. Suddenly I felt all alone inside."
"I cried, because I thought my parents had died."
"I couldn't breathe. I thought I was dying."
"The day I came here, I stopped living."

To the child separated from his family, it does feel like his parents have died, for death is the ultimate separation. The feelings of loss are like a pain deep inside: "It hurts, I mean it really hurts." Every child in placement goes through a process of mourning his lost (dead) parents, very much like an adult mourns the death of a loved one.

Though all children feel the pain, their reactions to it are varied, for how people respond to death is an individual matter. Our responses are shaped in part by our age, the feelings we had toward the person who died, how unexpected

Child: *This is my family. That's me and my brothers and sisters. My oldest sister is holding my new baby brother.*

Teacher: *Where are your parents?*

Child: *Boy are you stupid. My mother took the picture so she couldn't be in it.*

the death (separation) was, and whether or not we have had previous experiences with loss (death). When children are placed in foster care, they may act differently, but they *feel* the same.

One common reaction to the feeling of hurt and loss is to cry. Crying serves a double purpose; not only does it express how the child feels, it also is a call for the mother. Tears have a magic about them; they make mothers appear to see what is wrong. Crying with tears is the most obvious kind of crying. Some children only cry on the inside. They lie silently in the corner, legs drawn up, thumb in the mouth, fetus-like, hoping to be reunited with mother. Their face is a mask of sadness, but you don't see any tears. Maybe at night, when loneliness and being away from home are at their worst, they wet the bed. That can be a form of crying, too.

Some children actively protest their placement with a bellow of rage and indignation. Their language pollutes the air and their wrath is visited upon whomever or whatever is near at hand, be it foster parents, child care workers, furniture, or other children. Their actions speak loudly indeed: "When my parents see and hear how much I love them, they will change their minds and take me back."

One child interrupted a no-holds-barred, all-stops-out temper tantrum to ask a child care worker if her mother had come yet. When told that her mother was not expected, she picked up where she had left off, in the middle of a scream. They may cry or scream for hours or for days, or not at all, but when neither these nor other stratagems changes the reality of placement, despair sets in. The child's cry for help from Mommy and Daddy has been answered by silence.

Despair is pain, too, only it hurts more because now there isn't even the hope that the pain will stop. Human beings can't stand pain for very long, and if at all possible, they will run away from it. When you are a foster child, and there is no place to run to, then all that's left is to build a wall to keep the hurt away. Most foster children wall off the painful feelings of loss and despair by eventually resisting any discussion of home or their parents. To mention the parents is to feel pain. To know your parents are alive but that you can't have them is only adding insult to injury. Some of them will tell you what they feel is true anyway, that their parents are really dead.

The step from protest to despair follows a timetable unique to each child. For some it is a matter of days; for others hope dies more slowly and may linger on for months. Eventually the walling-off process is completed and the child arrives at a stage of detachment. He acts as if it doesn't matter that he has lost his parents. With his feelings hidden, a frozen smile on his face, he goes about his daily routine. Some say that he has settled in, finally accepted the separation from his parents. They are mistaken.

The loss of hope marks a withdrawal from the outside world. Reality has become too painful a place in which to live. There is another world, a far better place in which to live, a world where children and parents are together. It is an inner world that only its creator can see and experience — it is called fantasy.

It is to the fantasy world that the child now turns. It is a world made up largely of opposites of the painful outside world. In this world the hope still flickers that his parents will reclaim their own. Any day now, one or both of his parents will show up on his doorstep, smash down the barred doors, slay the evil jailer, and triumphantly sweep their lost child into their arms and carry him home. Any day now, just wait and see. Wait . . . and wait . . . and wait.

While the child is waiting, he puzzles over the question, "Why am I here?" Most children find an answer. It is known as the "no-good hypothesis," whose common form is the child's belief that "I am no good, something is terribly wrong with me, and that is why my parents sent me away."

That which is thrown away or abandoned is of little worth or significance. It is a very small step for the child to conclude that he is worthless and no good. Having arrived at this natural conclusion, the child begins to cast about inside of himself to see if he can find the specific badness in himself which led to his rejection by his parents. The age at which the separation takes place plays an important role in determining the answer the child finds. Most children conclude that the badness is the issue in their psychological development that they were struggling with at the time of their separation.

For example, a child who has a sibling born shortly before he himself is placed in foster care will likely conclude that his anger toward his mother and the new baby was the reason he had to be sent away. Another child, placed at one month of age, may well decide that he cried too much and his mother couldn't stand him, so she placed him. Another child, placed at the end of first grade, reasoned that his failure to be promoted had shamed his parents so that they no longer wanted to keep him.

Gradually, the child builds his own picture of his imagined badness until eventually he becomes convinced that it was his bad behavior, and solely this, that was responsible for his abandonment. Having an answer is usually satisfying in itself, but this particular answer provides an additional satisfaction. Up to now the child has felt himself the helpless victim of fate, insignificant, worthless, cast aside, and unable to control the forces that tore him from his parents. With the assumption of total blame for his placement, because of his bad behavior, he is no longer helpless. Nothing has happened to him — he *caused* it. Who can say it is not better to be a strong and bad somebody than a weak and good nobody? It is not an easy job to be the foster parent of a child who is convinced that he is a monster.

Some children can resolve their inner tensions by heaping badness upon themselves. For others, with different personalities, this is not a solution. These children direct their anger not toward themselves, but toward their parents. This alternative form of the no-good hypothesis would go: "My parents are no good, something is terribly wrong with them, and that's why I was sent away." It is usually the older children who will tell you openly what miserable, no-good parents they had. If you listen carefully, you can hear the qualification. "My parents are bad now, but I am hoping that any day now they will change for the better and take me back." Ironically, those children who hope for change the hardest are often the ones with the most inconsistent and rejecting parents. These children are constantly confused about what to expect from their parents. They mistakenly equate the changes of inconsistency with the potential for constructive change in the parents. As angry as the children who blame their parents are, most are willing to forgive and forget if only the parents would make restitution for all of the pain and deprivation they have caused, by taking them back home again.

A third form of the no-good hypothesis should be mentioned. It appears most commonly in adolescents, about thirteen to fifteen years of age, after they have been in care for a number of years. It is related to the adolescent's struggle for independence. It goes like this: "There is nothing wrong either with me or my parents. The trouble is that some no-good interfering social worker took me away from my parents. If only I could get back to my parents, everything would be all right." Of course, everything would not be all right if the child went home, and deep down the child knows this, but he struggles for independence from the evil and cruel people who are caring for him and idealizes his real parents and wants to run to them. It is not easy to raise an adolescent and it is even more difficult to raise one who is not your own.

"I don't have to do what you tell me to," they say; "you're not my real parents."

Even though all deprived and neglected children are angry at their parents for being neglectful or for loving them so little that they could give them up to a stranger, it is the exceptional child who can openly and consistently express this anger toward his parents. Right or wrong, good or bad, adequate or not, they are and always will be the child's natural parents and the focus of strong positive as well as negative feelings. The longer the child is away from his parents, the more the negative feelings diminish and the more the positive ones build, until they become idealized fantasies. The knowledge that one has lost one's "true" parents will always remain as a tender spot of pain on the psyche.

Most of the orphans of the living are extremely protective of their parents, a fact which, when one knows their histories, is very hard to understand. One thirteen-year-old girl, who wanted to leave placement to live with a married sister and was not allowed to do so because the sister neither wanted her nor could care for her, screamed her rage to her foster mother about her social worker instead.

"That damned social worker doesn't want me to be with my sister," she protested. "She said my sister can't care for her own baby, much less for me. She called my sister a no-good slut. She's got no right to talk about my sister that way. She's a slut, a slutty social worker, and the next time I see her I'm going to kill her for saying that."

But we are so much a part of our parents that to attack them is to vilify ourselves. To admit that they were neglectful is to affirm that we are worthy of neglect. To want to be other than like them is to aspire to be nobody at all. Again and again, children will cling to the old and destructive parent-child relationship rather than face the uncertainties of new relationships. There is not a child in placement who won't forever afterwards fear the wish to love and be loved, for with love are sowed the seeds of another rejection.

The child who is placed in foster care has severed a relationship with emotionally important people. This was necessary because of abuse and neglect of the child by the parents. This implies there was an inadequate relationship between parent and child in which the child's needs were not met adequately. It will come as no surprise, then, that the major difficulty of the child in placement is in his relationships with other people, especially caretakers, that is, foster parents, child care workers, teachers, social workers, and so on. Basically, the child will see these people as he saw his parents: he will expect them to act toward him as his parents acted; he will project onto them the same behavior, feelings, and motives that he experienced with his parents; he will bring to the relationships the same feelings that the parents aroused in him; in short, he will reproduce with these new people the pathological patterns that he had with his parents in the past.

He will do this, first, because how we relate to others is a consequence of learned patterns of behavior, shaped in the early formative years by our relationships with our parents. Secondly, the child will repeat his past because it is a form of defense for him; it helps him ward off painful situations and handle unacceptable feelings in the present. The more disturbed a child is, the more likely he is to rely upon past methods of mastery to deal with the present. Even the less disturbed children, will, at times of unmanageable stress, revert to old patterns of behavior.

It is precisely this difficulty in forming relationships that makes the job of child care worker in an institution or foster parent in a home so difficult and emotionally draining. The foster child in care is constantly testing adults, provoking them, attempting to play one adult against another, defying them, and generally attempting to manipulate the emotions and behavior of the adults to make his new "parents" match the unconscious picture of the old, lost parents that he carries in the wallet of his mind.

It is because this behavior goes on that it is so vitally important that these substitute parents be provided with casework or other consultative support in their efforts to deal with the child. The foster child, perhaps more than most children, is especially adept at picking out the chinks in the adult's emotional armor. When a foster child, trying to work out old problems of dealing with angry parents, hits upon that one spot of emotional tenderness in a foster parent that makes the adult mad, there is going to be fireworks. Without the support of a caseworker to clarify what is going on, the foster placement is likely to collapse.

Take for example, the case of Roger Soole, presented in

Chapter 1, the boy placed because of his mother's illness. After a short stay in a child care institution, the state welfare worker managed to move Roger into a foster home. The home was that of a young couple who had been married slightly over a year and who did not have any children of their own. Roger thrived under the individual attention he received and things went well for a number of months.

Then, as so often happens to these children, fate dealt Roger an unkind blow. The worst possible thing, from the point of view of Roger's emotional strength to handle it, happened. His foster mother became pregnant. She was thrilled by this development and in her naïve enthusiasm shared the news with Roger, whom she expected would also be thrilled.

Not so. Roger had been through all this when he was three. His mother had become pregnant and he had been placed! Roger knew what a new baby meant — it meant that he and his foster mother would be separated. Without a word, Roger went upstairs, packed his suitcase, and ran away. He was picked up that evening by the police and eventually returned to the foster home the next day, a frightened, anxious, and angry little boy. The foster mother sensed what was bothering him, and went to great pains to reassure him that they would not send him away when the new baby came. Roger seemed mollified.

As the pregnancy went on, the foster mother began to have morning sickness, was tired, short-tempered, and took to staying in bed more than usual. That behavior, too, seemed vaguely familiar to Roger, whose own mother had been ill and depressed. His anxiety increased and he made extreme demands for attention and care from the foster mother. Unable to meet these, she became increasingly irritated with him and began to express the need to be free from the responsibility of caring for him. The state welfare worker, had she known what was going on, might have been able to arrange a homemaker service, but she hadn't been to visit the foster home for three months.

Roger, however, saw the handwriting on the wall, and

even though too young to read, he sensed what it meant. The past was about to catch up to him and he would once again be separated from his "mother." His anger against his real mother welled to the surface, only this time he wasn't helpless to express it. While his foster mother was taking an afternoon nap, Roger stole into her bedroom and set the wastebasket on fire. The foster mother awoke in time to see one end of her bedroom engulfed in flames. (How familiar that must have seemed to Roger.)

The frightened foster mother called the fire department and the state welfare worker, in that order. Roger was returned to the child care center that very evening. It was a different boy who returned to the institution than the one brought kicking and screaming there nearly a year before under very similar circumstances. Roger walked in under his own power, calm and collected. When a worker expressed surprise at seeing him back, Roger shrugged and said, "I had to come back. My foster mother got burned up at a fire at our house."

Roger had learned how to cope with stress. When you know you are going to be rejected, reject them first. That way it doesn't hurt quite so much.

Sally Downe, the child with a psychotic mother, had been the victim of many of her mother's bizarre acts. She had good reason to be fearful and distrustful of the care that she would receive from adults. In spite of all the frightening things that happened to her when she was with her mother, there were strong, emotionally rewarding times in their relationship, too. Mrs. Downe had been very responsive to her daughter concerning the issue of meeting infantile needs. Though Sally was seven years old, mother fed her from a bottle, kept her in diapers which she lovingly changed, and did not allow Sally to leave her to go to school. When Sally acted like a baby, she received her mother's whole-hearted emotional interest. If she acted more grown up, she lost her mother, so Sally opted for being a baby and getting what she needed.

When Sally was admitted into care, she tried to reassure herself about the way these new people would act toward her by doing the things that elicited interest and involvement from her mother. She soiled herself, fully expecting the child care staff would delight in changing her. Sally also refused to feed herself and talk in anything other than baby talk.

Needless to say, the staff did not respond to her behavior with enthusiasm. They refused to feed her, insisting she could feed herself. (Reluctantly, Sally did.) They grumbled about changing her and replaced her diapers with panties, mildly rebuking her for messing herself and strongly hinting that a big girl like her could use the toilet. In this area, Sally did not give into the staff. Her soiling intensified; she soiled her pants in bed at night, during the day in school, during mealtimes at the table. She took her soiled pants off and hid them around the cottage, much to the distress of the staff. As the crowning blow, Sally left little piles of feces heaped on the floor next to the toilet bowl, pointedly refusing to deposit them where they belonged. All Sally's other babyish behavior disappeared, but this one symptom persisted. It was the last emotional link from the past between a little girl and her psychotic mother.

The persistence of Sally's symptom has important diagnostic implications. By observing a child's interactions with adults while in care, we can infer a good deal about how the child was treated by the parents and what the parent-child relationship was like. Conversely, if we know from the child's record about his past relationships with his parents, we can often predict what his relationship will be with the adults while in care. By anticipating the nature and type of difficulties he will have relating to substitute parents, we can act to support the foster parents and ease the child's adjustment problems.

The crucial thing is how ingrained those patterns of relating are. When substitute parents fail to respond as the natural parents did, the child who is able to modify his behavior somewhat is the one who is most likely to benefit from substitute care. The child, like Sally, who cannot modify but only intensifies her old patterns of behavior, is a child who is very difficult to help and who often fails to improve in substitute care. Those who benefit are those who eventually are able to realize that not all adults are like their parents were. Of course, no child changes his behavior the first time he meets a response from adults different from that of his natural parents. Instead, the child sets out unconsciously to manipulate the feelings of the adult to the point where the adult does respond in the way the parents did.

Phillip Myers, the boy placed by his mother in order to find out what was wrong with him, is an example of this. Phillip and his mother had been involved in an angry and destructive relationship. Mrs. Myers rejected Phillip because she saw him as being just like his abusive father. Failing to have his needs met, and angry at his mother, Phillip retaliated with hyperactive behavior and sadistic taunting of his little sisters. Eventually this led to the ultimate rejection, Phillip's placement in foster care.

At the child care institution, Phillip lived in a cottage with eighteen other boys, cared for by a cottage mother, but no father. Phillip's anger at his mother was readily shifted onto the cottage mother, and he continued his battle, provoking her by beating up the younger boys. When his behavior was met by understanding and firm discipline, without angry shouting and beatings, Phillip was puzzled. His whole concept of himself as the active provoker of mother's meanness was threatened. He wasn't ready to face the upsetting alternative to being the active agent (something must be wrong with my mother and there is nothing I can do about that), and intensified his provocative behavior.

He zeroed in on a young child care worker. She had patiently dealt with numerous incidents of Phillip's aggressive behavior toward younger children this particular day, and her patience was near the end. As she closed in on Phillip to break up a fight, he suddenly turned on her and kicked her in the shins.

"Get away from me," Phillip screamed. "I hate you. You're mean and selfish."

The worker had endured the same charges from Phillip many times before and they had not bothered her. But this time, his accusations took on a new meaning. The previous evening, she had broken up with her boyfriend following a heated argument. She had, in fact, treated him badly during the evening and he had finally exploded and called her a selfish bitch. Phillip's words cut her deeply, arousing her guilt and anger. Her involuntary and unthinking response was to deliver a stinging slap across Phillip's mouth. She was horrified at her reaction but Phillip's face broke into a smile and his rage disappeared.

"I knew you were mean," he said; "you hit kids." He turned on his heel and walked away, leaving a stunned worker behind.

Phillip was comfortable again. Before, his anger had no basis in the present — he had been met by kindness and understanding. Now, after the slap, he was justified in feeling angry with his worker. She was mean and she had hit him. His view of the world was confirmed: mothers were mean and abusive.

There are, of course, other aspects to Phillip's behavior — other needs that are satisfied by being angry with his worker. It has been said that every child in placement both wishes for and fears emotional closeness to others. Phillip found that he was beginning to like the child care worker and wishing to be close to her. In the past, closeness had led to separation and hurt, so the closer Phillip became to the worker, the more anxious and fearful he felt. One very common way children have of warding off closeness is to make the adult angry. This usually leads to withdrawal and rejection of the child. The child then blames the adult for being angry at him, avoiding facing his own anger at the "parents" and his own part in pushing people away.

Children in placement expect to be rejected. They may hope for acceptance, but they expect rejection, because it happened to them once and was so traumatic and incapable of being mastered. They remain forever sensitive to the possibilities of separation in any new situation. Sometimes the anxiety of waiting for the expected to happen becomes so intolerable that the child literally brings it upon himself; he makes the worst possible thing happen. When it does, he can breathe a sigh of relief, as if to say, "There, now I can relax, the worst has happened."

Mary was a teen-ager in group placement. Her class at school was to go on a field trip. The morning before they left, Mary's behavior at school was impossible. She fought with other children, provoked the teacher, swore loudly, tipped over chairs, and so on. Finally, the teacher, fearing that Mary was too upset this day to go on the trip, told her she would have to stay behind. Mary quieted down for the rest of the morning. When it came time to get on the bus, she went out with the class. The teacher refused to let her on and the bus driver shut the door and drove off, leaving Mary behind. She chased the bus for half a block and then gave up. Abandoned once again, Mary went into a rage. She went back into her classroom and started smashing everything in sight, swinging a chair at the windows and kicking or throwing whatever she could lay her hands on. Another teacher, passing by the classroom, intervened to stop her.

As he held Mary to restrain her from breaking things, she screamed out, "I knew this would happen. I knew yesterday something would happen to keep me from going on this trip."

The teacher still didn't know quite what had happened, but Mary's comment was enough to make him suspect that Mary had in some way provoked a rejection. Before he could say anything, Mary started yelling again.

"That bitch. That no-good bitch. She hates me. I knew she wouldn't take me with her."

"You mean your teacher?"

"My mother," Mary replied unexpectedly. Suddenly tears were streaming down her cheeks as she crumpled to the floor in a heap. She flopped there, crying and moaning to herself, rocking back and forth and mumbling, "That no-good bitch of a mother of mine doesn't want me."

Mary had indeed provoked the teacher into leaving her behind. Being left behind awakened all the hidden feelings from the past. The teacher who restrained her from breaking up the room may have been puzzled by what had happened, but Mary knew at whom she was angry and what it was that she had really lost. For Mary, as with most children in placement, the emotional step from a present rejection to the past one is but a matter of inches.

The Kelley children, mentioned in Chapter 1 as a case of child abuse, were taken into care at a child care center. Four-year-old Kelly Kelley went first to a foster home, but that placement collapsed because of the foster mother's inability to tolerate Kelly's hyperactive and destructive behavior. So Kelly also ended up in the institution with her siblings. Her behavior there revealed yet another pattern of children's reactions to placement and separation.

At first, Kelly was very quiet and withdrawn, spending much time sitting in a corner sucking her thumb. After a few weeks, she began to be hyperactive and destructive. The staff found ways to deal with this and soon Kelly stopped breaking up things.

She spent much of her time out in the play yard and the staff noted she was rather reckless in her play. She ran in front of other children on the swings and dangled perilously from the jungle gym. It was on the jungle gym that she had her first accident. She slipped from the top and landed headfirst on the asphalt. She was knocked unconscious, had a slight concussion, and two horrendous black eyes for a month afterward.

These had barely returned to normal when Kelly fell off her bike and lacerated her knee. A week later, she stepped in front of a child swinging a baseball bat and opened a twelve-stitch wound in her scalp. Four months later, she broke her arm in a sledding accident.

It wasn't for any lack of supervision that Kelly was being injured. She was an accident-prone child. She was poorly coordinated, threw herself about with abandonment, took careless chances, and had a knack for being in the wrong place at the wrong time — a victim waiting for an accident to happen. She was constantly sick with colds, mainly from running out into the snow without galoshes or playing outside in the cold without a coat on. The staff were constantly after her to put on a coat before going out into freezing weather.

Frequently children who are abused or neglected by their parents seem to have an unconscious need to get themselves hurt. Sometimes the need isn't so unconscious. Some children in care will throw temper tantrums and in the process will pull out their own hair, beat their heads against the floor, and lacerate their skin with their fingernails. When this sort of self-injury occurs, a check of the child's background often shows that this is a child who was battered by his parents.

The need to hurt themselves stems from the intense anger these children have toward their parents for maltreating them, which arouses in the child an expectation that the parents will retaliate against them for that anger. Sometimes the child brings an injury on himself to avoid this fearful, fantasized punishment expected from the parents. Children who blame themselves for the separation from their parents often see injuries as the just punishment due them for their bad behavior. Then, too, children who have never been adequately cared for by adults do not develop a sense of their own worth. Not having been protected by adults, they never learn to value and protect themselves. They do unto themselves as was done unto them. These are the things that little girls like Kelly are made out of — anger, guilt, self-punishment, cuts, bruises, and broken bones.

There may be some hope that Kelly will survive to grow up. After her last accident, she confided to the nurse, "You know, this is a nice place. They care about you when you hurt." Or could Kelly have meant, "The only time people care about you is when you are hurt"?

Mark Hansen, the last case in Chapter 1, provides an extreme example of the use of fantasy to answer the question of why a child is in placement. While things may happen to us in this life because they happen, the human mind sees events in dramatic terms, that is, things happen for a reason. Man's social history as well as his personal life are attempts to answer the question of why certain things happened. We seem incapable of believing that events do not have to be caused, and if there is no obvious causal agent apparent, then the mind invents one. Sometimes it seems like reality is but an empty screen upon which we project our interpretation of that which we have never seen.

Mark, who was illegitimate, never saw his father and was separated forever from his mother when he was two years old. As he himself expressed it, in an autobiography he wrote, "I can't think of my mother's name or my father's name now because I haven't seen them for so many years."

Mark's mother was retarded and had been cared for most of her life in a state school. In Mark's mind, this place became a special hospital, where his mother was because she was sick. According to him, "a couple of days after I was born, my mother became ill." Does Mark think this is a cause-and-effect relationship, that his birth made his mother ill?

Lest anyone jump to that hasty conclusion, Mark adds, "My mother got sicker because my father left her. He didn't want anything to do with my mother when she was sick, so he took off." In Mark's mind, then, one clear and obvious result of separation is to make you get sick. Mark has been separated four times now, from both his natural parents and both of his foster parents. He is a boy who was born and then raised for the first two years of his life in the infirmary of a state school. True, he was born with a number of congenital complications and the suspicion of mental retardation. He spent much of his early life in the foster home going in and out of hospitals for various tests, minor surgery, and diagnostic studies. In recent years, he has been not so much physically sick as fearful of a unique kind of illness, being poisoned. Mark thinks people are trying to poison him. In his fantasy, he believes he was nursed by a sick mother, who gave him some sickness through her poisoned milk. He is convinced something is wrong with him, that he is different from others, peculiar-looking in some way. This idea has an important correlate. Since separation makes people sick, the opposite is also true, that is, sickness makes people separate. Mark did say that his father ran away because his mother was sick, but it was only much later that he revealed another of his fantasies, that the day after his birth, his father came into the nursery and saw him in his crib, and *then* he ran away. Mark believes that he was so strange-looking that he scared away his own father. When Mark told this terrible thought of his, he broke down and cried, and asked in an anguished voice, "What *is* wrong with me?"

Mark is the monster who scared away his own father and made his mother sick, but as often happens, these unacceptable ideas are reversed in fantasy. It was his mother who made him sick with her poisoned milk, and his father who scares him. Mark has terrible nightmares in which a strange man sneaks into his bedroom and tries to choke him. Sometimes in the dark and lonely nights he hears a voice calling to him. He sees the faint figure of a man beckoning to him and he gets out of bed. Suddenly he is afraid. Is it his lost father who wants him back, or is it a monster who will lure him outside and kill him? Horrible thoughts of gory mutilations rush through his head and he can't decide whether to follow the man or run away. He feels himself grow dizzy and he faints. When he wakes up, he is lying on the floor in a tangle of bed sheets, and he is alone. Mark cries, because he is alone and doesn't understand what is happening.

Once he wrote a poem in which he expressed his feelings of being alone.

> Loneliness is missing somebody
> who never said good-bye.
> And now I have no place to go —
> I'm lonely 'til I die.

In one of his dreams, Mark thought he heard someone call him by another name. From this one brick, he built a whole house where he now lives. You see, there was this mix-up in the hospital and Mark was really kidnaped by his foster parents and for all those years his real parents were searching for him. They are fine people, healthy, strong, and good-looking, filled with a great sadness for their lost son and a deep love for him. If there weren't this conspiracy by the state welfare worker to keep Mark away from his parents, they would find him and take him away to live with them.

There is, of course, much more to the story, but you wouldn't believe it. It sounds too much like a very bad melodramatic novel. But then, reality makes very poor fiction, and fiction supposedly apes reality, which does make things confusing. In reality, Mark is lonely; in his fantasy, he is a real, live person.

There are those who would say that Mark is psychotic and perhaps they are right, though not in the usual sense. Psychosis is usually seen as a regression of the ego under stress to a much more infantile level of thinking, feeling, and functioning. Mark hasn't regressed because he never progressed much to begin with. His early formative years were ones of such deprivation that Mark never developed emotionally; he was emotionally stunted. Which means that the issues of development that he is currently struggling with are those of the very young child, issues of basic trust,

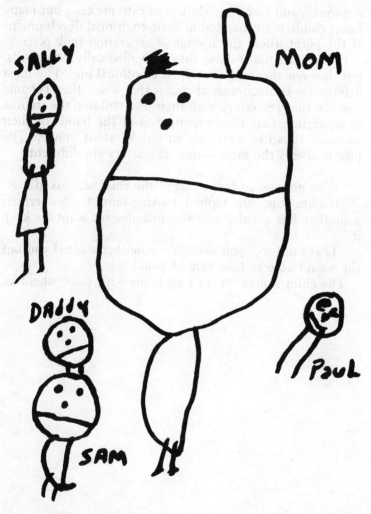

Daddy is standing on top of Sam's head — a family picture
by a five-year-old. Note relative size of mother

self-worth, and identity. Mark is an extreme case, but many foster children are arrested in their emotional development at the point where the trauma of separation took place.

In the years that follow, they grow physically into adults, but they remain children in their emotional life. The most deleterious consequence of this is that when they become parents, they reproduce with their own children the trauma of separation that they experienced at the hands of their parents. It is like watching an old Western movie. The plot is always the same — only the actors are different.

"Why are you in foster care?" the child was asked.

"It's like this," she replied, looking serious. "Sometimes a mother has a baby and she just doesn't want to keep it."

"That's not so," you say. "Your mother wanted you but she wasn't able to take care of you."

The child smiles. "Can I go home with you?" she asks.

3

Who Am I?

"The thing I dislike most in the world is myself."

— A CHILD IN FOSTER CARE.

"My Dad is the greatest. I want to grow up to be just like him.

"On second thought, maybe he's a bum, in which case I don't want to grow up to be like him.

"Actually, I haven't seen my father in eight years, so how can I know if I want to grow up to be like him or not?"

— A TEN-YEAR-OLD BOY IN CARE.

Picture drawn by an eight-year-old foster child (girl) for her social worker

The most pervasive, chronic problem of the child in foster care is his poor self-concept. A child's concept of himself is built up slowly over time, forged out of many life experiences and complicated interactions with a variety of people. It is the sum total of all that the child can call his: body, mind, clothes, parents, siblings, house, name, friends, toys, school, relatives, reputation, pets, money, memories, all that he has made, and so forth. One's concept of self can be broken down into many interrelated parts. This chapter will focus on three: feelings of self-worth, feelings of self-competence, and a sense of self-identity, examining each of them more closely in terms of the child in foster care.

Feelings of Self-Worth

Feelings of self-worth have to do with one's estimate of oneself as a worthwhile and lovable person. Normally, a child comes to think of himself well because he was loved and cared for consistently by his parents. A child removed from his parents not only wasn't getting this love and care essential to developing a sense of worth, but he loses any possibility of getting it from his parents as long as he is away from them. It matters not that he wasn't getting it and wouldn't get it; what matters is that the child sees this as a further deprivation.

In the previous chapter, the psychological process by which the child attempts to understand this separation was elaborated. He concludes that he was rejected because of some bad behavior on his part. He comes to believe that he is bad and unlovable and goes on to recreate this role of the bad child in his relationships with the new adults who care for him. That which began as an explanation for his rejection now becomes a part of his character: the child *feels* that he is bad. The unfortunate part is that almost all of what will happen to the child after his placement only reinforces his negative evaluation of his own worth.

That he is placed and not living with his parents — in fact, doesn't have parents in the sense that other children have them — gives the child in foster care a sense of being different (that is, bad). Unfortunately in our society, we are unable to make a distinction between things without at the same time making value judgments about that difference. Anything normal is good, while deviations of almost any kind are automatically bad. In a society which supposedly values individual freedom, we have an unholy fear of anything that is different. The minute a child is separated from his family, he becomes different and that sense of difference remains with the child throughout his entire life. It is not uncommon to talk with the parents of a child who has been placed and have them blurt out during the interview, "I'm not like other people you know.

When I was a child, I was on the state." Years later that difference still rankles them, because no one was there to help work through their loss as children.

The loss of parents is trauma enough, but for many children it is only the beginning. Hasty placements, poor selection of foster parents, inadequate supervision and support of foster parents, and poorly trained state welfare workers all result in an increasingly high number of foster home placement failures. Children are moved from one placement to another, to a different foster home or eventually to a child care institution. The people who deal with these children cannot understand and do not accept the child's disturbed behavior. Hostility toward others, the most common symptom of the abused and neglected child, is seen as ingratitude by uninformed foster parents and child care workers and not as a sign that the child is hurting inside. When the child acts out his bad self-concept, to see if he is acceptable, he finds instead that he is unloved and rejected once again by the foster parents who demand his removal from their home. No matter how this is handled with the child, the stigma is always on him, never the foster parents. He has been removed from the placement because of his bad behavior. Whenever anything goes wrong, he is the one to suffer, for it is he who must leave. One child expressed this vulnerability quite clearly in these words.

"Whenever I did something wrong, I would be punished. The worst punishment was not a whipping, or no TV, or not going out to play, it was having to move again. I was always afraid that I would have to move again."

The foster child is not allowed to express how he feels to the degree that a normal child is. Some feelings, especially aggression, must be kept under tight control if he wants to remain in placement. After a while, the continued presence of these unacceptable feelings and the struggle to control them give the child the impression that he is bad to have these thoughts and feelings. The pressure on the child not to let them out builds up. He never learns how to handle them because he is prevented from working them through in an accepting atmosphere.

Another child in placement graphically described this sense of pressure. "I always thought twice before I did say anything, to be sure I didn't say the wrong thing. As a result, I talk very slowly, which makes people mad at me." Even when he tried to do the right thing, he was wrong.

Another child described the need to please the foster parents and how difficult it was to do this and still be a child. In speaking of his many foster home placements before coming into institutional care, he said:

"First I was in a home with the Smiths, but they didn't like a lot of noise, so I had to leave there. Next it was the Browns. She had a baby a few months after I came there and there wasn't any room for me, so I left there. Then it was the Joneses. She didn't like me at all so I went to the Harrises. I guess they couldn't stand something about me either, so here I am here with you."

Not all children act out their role as the bad child. Some, while still believing it about themselves, try very hard to be very good. You can almost "see" their reason for making this concerted effort. If it was because of their bad behavior that they lost their parents, then the way to get them back is to be good, so they'll want to take you back. One little girl in placement in a child care center exhibited model behavior for months, only to fall apart when her best friend was discharged.

"It's not fair," she screamed. "I've been here much longer than she has and besides, I've been good. She broke her toys and talked back to people and screamed. Mothers don't like children who scream." How do you help a child accept that whether you behave well or not, it has nothing to do with coming into placement or staying there?

Any child who doesn't have emotional needs met over a period of time comes to feel badly about himself. The child in foster care, because his relationships with adults are impaired, has great difficulty experiencing satisfying emotional relationships. Interactions tend to result in frustration, pain, anger, rejection, and disappointment. He has not learned how to establish and maintain satisfying relationships. He needs a stable relationship in which to learn how.

Tragically, few of his relationships are stable. Frequent placement moves have already been mentioned as a cause, but even if the child stays in one place, the people in his environment frequently move. Social workers appear and disappear with frightening regularity; child care workers have a high rate of turnover in institutions (low status, poor wages, split shifts including evenings and weekends, and lack of in-service training programs are some of the variables associated with this turnover); and all too often there is no family worker assigned to his case to work toward rehabilitating his parents. Other foster children in care with him come and go on an unpredictable basis. His parents are highly erratic, most often not visiting at all, or even worse, promising to visit him and then never showing up when they say they will. A child may hear nothing from his parents for months, then out of the blue will come a birthday card or Christmas present, and then nothing for months. It is virtually impossible for a child to come to accept the separation from his parents and deal with the loss if they are going to reappear erratically. Either the parents must be helped to visit frequently, or if the contact cannot be maintained after a reasonable period of time, then for the child's emotional health it should be irrevocably severed. The on-again, off-again contact with chronically inadequate parents wreaks havoc with the child's mental health, especially with his self-identity.

More than anything, the entire quality of care provided the neglected and dependent child by the state reinforces his low estimate of his self-worth. If we do not care enough to provide the child with quality care, we should not be surprised if he comes to believe that he is worthless. (See the discussion of the value society places on children in Chapter 5.) As one child put it, "My parents don't want me. Nobody loves me or cares what happens to me." Another child clinched it with, "Do you know who I am? I'm nobody's nothing."

Feelings of Self-Competency

When a child is able actively to master his environment, he comes to see himself as a competent person. There is a very close relationship between feeling competent and feeling worthwhile. Children are secure when they feel competent. All children in growing up face developmental tasks peculiar to each stage of development. Some of these tasks include developing a sense of trust in others; a sense of autonomy; initiative; self-control (including the ability to delay gratification of impulses); and an identification with one's parents. Normally a child masters each of these successive developmental challenges and in so doing comes to feel that he is competent, able actively to master his world.

The child in foster care faces these same challenges in development but with one very important difference. His struggles for mastery take place within the context of an overwhelming emotional stress, namely, the separation from his parents. This additional stress tips the balance against the likelihood that he will master the subsequent developmental tasks adequately. All too often the child's emotional development is frozen at the level on which he functioned when separation took place. His subsequent failure to master developmental tasks and the absence of consistent parental love and care seriously undermine his sense of competence and self-worth.

The author of one study[1] described dependent institutionalized children: "They showed little faith in themselves and in their prospects for a pleasant, successful future life; they were seriously demoralized."

The two words used to describe these children were "demoralized" and "depersonalized" — another way of saying that they had problems in self-esteem and self-identity.

Sometimes those who see these children briefly in benign

settings find it hard to believe that they are children with psychological problems. They are fooled by the superficial friendliness and seeming outgoingness of the children. If their contact was longer, they would find children who did not trust adults; those older children who cling excessively to the adult in helpless dependency; those whose liveliness and curiosity have been stifled; those who demand to be given an endless supply of material things; those whose anger rages out of control at the slightest provocation; those who have no sense of who they are. Whenever children fail to develop physically, mentally, or emotionally, their sense of competence is diminished. They end up feeling, "I can't do that, I don't know how." When the foster child says this, he means, "Nobody cared enough to help me learn how to do that."

Children, like adults, feel competent when they are able to be of help to others. Whenever a person is put in the position where he is always the one who receives care and is never given opportunities to do for others, his competency is undermined. We forget that even the needy want to be needed. Children are no longer an economic necessity to the family as they once were when we were an agrarian society. They are needed in less tangible ways and, unless we are careful, we give them the impression that their only purpose is to be objects of care. We should not be surprised under these circumstances if in adolescence they turn out to be egocentric and expect that they should be given to all the time rather than also to give to others. How even more true for the foster child, who is "in care."

One adolescent in his natural family was asked by his parents to help by taking out the trash every week. The boy fussed and complained, an argument ensued, and one of the parents finally said in exasperation, "Do you think we're asking too much of you around here?"

The boy stormed off in a huff without answering. Three hours later, when he had cooled off, he returned, pulled up a chair, and said to his parents, "No, I don't think that's too much to ask of me. I don't know why I complain. I just can't help myself. If you really want to know the truth, I don't think you ask enough of me."

That is not to suggest that children should be put to work in foster homes or in institutions, but rather that we should strive to create opportunities for them to be able to help others, to be needed by someone. Perhaps what we need is not so much foster care as it is foster caring.

Another aspect of the problem is that it is very difficult to feel competent if you are always completely helpless to control any of the things that happen to you. Typically, the child in foster care has his life disordered without knowing about it in advance and without having any part in deciding what will happen to him. He is taken from his parents, placed, moved, replaced, kept an indeterminate length of time, and has his future discussed by strangers who supposedly have his best interests at heart. Granted, many children are too young or immature to make decisions about their life, but there are other ways of helping them feel less helpless about what happens to them. We know it is important to the child's well-being that he be prepared for major changes in his life. One doesn't just whisk a child away from his parents into foster care, or tell a child in an institution that he is to leave the next morning to go to a foster home. There needs to be time to get used to the idea of the change; a time to say good-bye to friends and parents; a time to express resentment, anger, and fear; a time to think of what objects from the past he wants to take with him; a time to visit the new place a few times and gradually integrate and accept what will become the reality. We know this and yet most of the time placements are made precipitously without planning because it is an "emergency" situation, or it is easier for the adults, or our own anxieties impel us to action. (A typical reaction of welfare workers who are leaving their jobs is to try to "settle permanently" all of their children before they leave, more to ease the worker's anxiety and guilt than for the welfare of the child. After they've gone, the placements frequently collapse, but the ex-worker doesn't know about that. The new worker comes on the job to be overwhelmed at once at finding most of his cases in crisis.)

Even older children are rarely made part of the conferences at which their fate is decided. Even if they had no decision-making role, the children could still benefit from being included to hear the process by which decisions about them are made. The more ways we find to isolate them from what is happening to them and why, the more helpless and incompetent they feel.

The most clear-cut and institutionalized way society has of making the foster child (and a large number of other children as well) feel incompetent is the school system. The typical foster child's experience with the school is to feel frustrated, stupid, humiliated, angry, and incompetent. Schools, which could be emotionally remedial and supportive environments, as well as places where children's egos are strengthened, instead function to destroy the foster child's concept of himself as competent.

The traumatic and unstable family environments from which these children come, and the emotional conflicts resulting from their separation from their families, make these children emotionally unable to learn.[2] To learn from adults, the child must first trust the adult and see adults as positive, helpful, and supportive people. These children do not see their parents this way and do not transfer onto teachers, as do normal children, the positive qualities that promote learning. Instead, they bring to the learning relationship with the teacher feelings of anger, distrust of adults, suspicion, negativism, and open hostility.

The school, rather than seeing their educational task with these children as getting them emotionally ready to learn by providing an atmosphere of acceptance, trust, support, and helpfulness, responds by openly rejecting the foster child, as they do all children who do not learn in the one way that most schools teach. The children are labeled as learning and/or behavior problems. The school demands that the children change to fit the system, and when they do not, the system will not change to fit them. Instead they are banished from the system, either by suspending them from school entirely or by dispatching them to the room in the basement behind the boiler which is reserved as a special education classroom for emotionally disturbed children. The school may call what goes on there "special education" or remediation (often another illusion of caring), but instead it too often in fact is the expression of the attitude, "We have given up on you. You cannot learn."

Many foster children do not act out their problems in the classroom but instead retreat into fantasy. They do not disturb the routine of most classrooms, but neither do they learn. Since this type of student doesn't call attention to himself by disruptive behavior, he is frequently overlooked. Many teachers would not even realize that this behavior could indicate serious emotional difficulty. The following example of such a child shows what schools could do if they cared enough.[3]

Johnny, a depressed, withdrawn, and lonely boy, was failing all of his fifth-grade courses in spite of average intelligence. The enforced passivity of the classroom drove him deeper and deeper into his daydreams. His teacher could not penetrate his polite, detached, overly compliant behavior. As he was doing nothing in the classroom, Johnny was asked to tutor three first-graders for an hour a day in reading. He accepted this job without comment.

Soon, apathetic Johnny turned into a clock watcher. When his time came to tutor, he quietly slipped out of the classroom to go to the first grade. His enthusiastic pupils were so quiet and well behaved that the first-grade teacher scarcely knew they were in the room. After a few months, the group showed substantial progress under his instruction.

Johnny, the daydreamer, was never preoccupied while he tutored. His full attention was always on his students. Soon he showed an increased interest in his subjects in his own classroom. By the end of the year, his teacher knew that she was able to reach Johnny and that he was learning, at least some of the time.

The foster child's educational problems stem largely from motivational and behavioral difficulties, such as restlessness, hyperactivity, short attention span, distrust of adults, and generalized anger toward the world. Older children are often behind in grade placement and one or more years below their proper reading level. They are often verbally inarticulate and unable to express clearly both their thoughts and their feelings. Years of frustration and failure in school combine to produce in them an apathy toward learning. All these factors create special teaching difficulties.

Intruding into efforts at intellectual achievement is their constant preoccupation with thinking about their home and parents. One first-grade boy, trying to learn how to read, was struggling through a Dick and Jane story in which the children were in the kitchen with their mother, baking cookies. The boy suddenly burst into tears, and when the startled teacher asked him why he was crying, the boy replied: "My mother never did nice things with me like the mother in these stories does."

Another frequent intrusion into the academic work of foster children is the theme of aggression and injury. Here is an example in the composition of a seventh-grade boy who wrote his thoughts about a piece of artwork he had made.

Look at the colors. There are a lot of colors. I wonder how all the color starts. It must be different materials that are used, or maybe iridescence and shapes. Shapes are funny. They move all over the place without breaking up. Sometimes they are broken up into different pieces or lines. How come shapes don't cry when they are broken up? I cry when I get broken up. I almost got broken up one time by my father when I knocked over a fish tank. I stepped on the fishes. I don't like to kill fishes because they are pretty. Some fishes bite. My brother bites. He bites me. It hurts. I always get hurt. I get lots of cuts. I cut paper into small pieces and paste them on paper and make pretty colors and

shapes for art class. Talking about shapes, how come they
don't cry when they get broken up? I do.

Yet another example of this preoccupation with destruction, injury, and death comes from a poem written by a
foster child in an English class.

SNOWFLAKES

Snowflakes on my windows,
Snowflakes on my steps.
Snowflakes on my garden,
Kill my flowers to death.

The preoccupations of foster children with such themes
are learned attitudes about their world and what they believe are the important things that happen in it. Many
of these learned attitudes directly interfere with what we
call academic learning. School has always been a place for
the intellect, not for the emotions. But before many foster
children can learn academically, they must unlearn old attitudes and ways of handling emotions that interfere with
learning. Schools could be a place where unlearning and
relearning are encouraged. They could, if they became
more humane places. What we *don't* need are special
schools or special classes for the foster child. What we *do*
need are general schools where each child is special and
all children can experience success, develop to the limits
of their abilities, and feel good about themselves by discovering that they can be competent.

Feelings of Self-Identity

In their study of four hundred children in foster care, *Children in Need of Parents,* Maas and Engler reported that
only 10 to 23 percent of the children in the study were
judged to have a clear sense of self-identity.[4] Long-term
placement, especially when it begins at a young age, involves

a gradual erosion of parental ties, severely impairing the foster child's sense of identity. It is not the loss of the parents per se that causes the trouble, but rather the child's inability to resolve that loss.

Self-identity can be considered on many different levels, and perhaps the simplest answer to the question of "Who am I?" — at least for the young child — is his social history, that is, defined in terms of belonging to his parents and a family. The child's last name is a tangible sign of that belonging. (Some children in placement, confused about their identity, think their last name changes with each new family they go to live with.)

The more a child is cut off from knowledge of his early history, the less he feels like a real person. He doesn't know who he is because he has no sense of where he came from, no way to relate to his past. A teen-age boy who was placed when he was two, drew up a list of questions that he wanted answered about his past that illustrates this loss of self as a person.

1. What hospital was I born in? What was my birth weight? At what time of day was I born?
2. Are there any old pictures of me when I was small?
3. What did my parents do for a living? Are there any pictures of them in my record?
4. Do I have brothers and sisters? Any close relatives, like uncles or aunts?
5. Do I have any godparents? Who witnessed my baptism?
6. Do I have a middle name?
7. What were the names of some of my foster parents in the homes I lived in? My doctors? My teachers? My social workers?
8. Was I sick a lot as a child? What sicknesses did I have? Did I have any accidents or broken bones?
9. Why did I have to leave all the places I was in and why am I here?
10. Do I belong to anybody?

As far as this boy was concerned, his entire life history was a blank and so was he. There was nothing to which he could anchor himself. Keeping the child in touch with his past is one function of the family caseworker. Some do a good job of this and the child has a photograph of his parents, of himself and siblings, a favorite toy from home, and current information about his parents' welfare. For some children there are even regular visits from natural parents. Weinstein found out that continuing contact with natural parents was important for a child's adjustment in placement. It not only ameliorated the detrimental consequences of long-term foster care but also gave these children a higher sense of well-being than those children who were not visited.[5]

But for many children there is no family worker. Shortages of personnel in the state welfare departments and high case loads mean that many children get either a bare minimum of service or are uncovered entirely. Then there is no one to inform them of what is happening with their parents. Maas and Engler found almost half of the children in care in their sample were visited rarely or never by their natural parents.[6] It is clear that the parents of many of the children in this book are incapable of visiting. The whereabouts of some aren't known; others are psychologically incapable of translating a love for the child into a concrete action like visiting, even when it is for the welfare of the child.

It is the child who is cut off from his parents for an indefinite, unknown length of time who suffers the most damage to his self-identity. Though he has parents to whom he belongs, he is not with them; those that he is with take care of him, but he does not belong to them. Therein lies his identity dilemma — he is, in effect, nobody's child.

Such a child, a boy of six, decided to run away from the child care center where he was in placement because he got mad when a worker told him he had to brush his teeth before going to bed. He left his cottage and ran off toward the woods. On the way he met another staff member.

A MONSTER
— *drawn by a seven-
year-old boy*

"Where are you going?" the staff member asked.

"I'm running away," the boy said.

"I'm sorry to hear that. Be sure to be back by supper-time."

"OK," the boy said and ran off into the woods. The staff member went on into the cottage. Half an hour later, at suppertime, since the boy had not yet returned, he stepped outside to see if the child was in sight. As he stood there looking, the boy popped up from behind a nearby rock.

"Here I am," he called. "This is where I'm hiding in case anybody's looking for me."

What a sad thing to be afraid to run away because you don't belong to anyone and to believe that there just might not be anybody who would look for you. Children who live with their natural parents may run away *from* home, but foster children run *to* home, often to a fantasy of loving and caring parents who don't exist. One girl, whose mother had deserted her, constantly wandered away from the institution where she was in care and would become lost in the surrounding neighborhood. When asked why she was always wandering off, she replied, "I'm looking for my 'really' mother."

Another level of self-identity involves incorporating the values of the parents and wanting to become like them. The desire of a little child to become like his parents is very strong, but the parents in this book are not very attractive models of adulthood. If the child cannot become like the most important people in his life, then whom is he to become?

After a group therapy session, two adolescent girls in foster care at a children's institution sat around in the kitchen of their cottage, drinking Coke, eating cookies, and discussing the just completed session where they had talked about parents.

"Your mother sounds even meaner than mine," said one.

"She's not so bad when she doesn't drink," replied the other.

"I couldn't believe it when you told about how your father tried to, you know, fool around with you like that. Mine used to try to get in bed with me all the time. I never told my social worker about that. I was too ashamed. I thought I was the only girl in the world that had something disgusting like that happen to me."

"We've got great parents," the other agreed morosely.

There was a thoughtful period of silence, then one said, "Did you ever think of ending it? I mean like putting your head in the oven or something like that?"

"Hey, have you thought of that too? I wouldn't like to die by drowning or hanging — that'd be terrible — but I've thought of using a knife on my arms or something."

The other girl screwed up her face. "Ugh. That would be too messy."

"Sometimes I think I'd rather die than have to grow up. I keep thinking, what if I turn out to be just like her?"

"Does that bother you, too? That's when I think of killing myself. I'd hate to turn out like my mother."

"Do you think we have to be like them? Christ, I wouldn't want to be like my father, either. He's some kind of a pervert."

"I don't know. I ask myself the same question. Do I have to be like either of my parents?"

The answer to that question may seem obvious to us. "Of course you don't have to become like your parents. Why not become like a foster parent, or a cottage mother, or a child care worker, or an admired teacher, or your social worker?" After all, don't normal children want to imitate other adults besides their parents?

The trouble with this obvious answer to the child's question is that things just don't work that way. The answer is based on a myth, on outmoded, simplistic ideas about the impact of external environment on the child. We act as if we need only remove a child from an unhealthy environment and place him in a more healthy one and there will be nothing to prevent him from wanting to become like the people who now take care of him. Surrounded by caring adults and character-building influences, we believe he will forget his poor experiences with his parents and rush to embrace mental health. Give him the proper training to make up for what he didn't get, develop some good habits of character, and he will grow up to be an adequate, independent, self-fulfilled adult.

This is perhaps the most insidious part of the illusion of caring. It is the attitude: "Look at all we are doing for these children. We spend millions of dollars to take them out of bad environments and maintain them in foster care. With that large an expenditure, how can they help but turn out well?" Spending money can be another illusion of caring; it looks like we are really doing something useful. We believe that the more money we spend, the better the product we get, whether this is education, health care, foster care, or new cars. Often this assumption about quality is not justified.

More often than not, our social welfare programs concentrate on highly visible changes that help promote the illusion that we are doing something about the problem. When we take a child out of a bad environment, people can see this is a good thing to do. But we confuse this necessary action with having solved the problem. Having removed the child from the environment, it can no longer adversely affect him. What we don't see, what we seldom attend to, and what in the end makes all the millions we spend on maintenance a farce, is the invisible, but nonetheless real, inner world of the child. Physical removal from the parents does not end the parental influences on a child. The parent-child relationship lives on, hidden in the child's mind. Like the germs of syphilis, this relationship lies dormant, to erupt at a later age and wreak havoc. The time of eruption frequently coincides with the onset of adolescence in the child.

All children have intensely ambivalent feelings toward their parents. They both love and hate them, admire and are jealous of them, wish to become like them and wish to replace them. This conflict of tensions between opposing emotions is usually resolved in the normal child, given the consistent, loving care of stable parents. But with the foster child, the disruption of the parent-child relationship and the parental instability act to block the child's resolution of the conflict.

Instead, for the foster child, love and hate become intensified. The desire to love and be loved by the parents grows because it is unsatisfied. The hate for the parents is fed by the additional resentment of being placed, that is, not loved enough to be cared for by the parents. As these two opposing feelings become stronger, it is increasingly difficult for the child to resolve them and the more anxious, uncomfortable, and guilty he becomes. The problem is feeling two opposite ways about the same objects (the parents) and, since the conflict can't be resolved, many children arrive at a way to sidestep it. They split the feelings into separate parts and attach each feeling to a different object, that is, they now feel only one way about each of two objects. Concretely, what most often happens is that the love centers on the lost parents (to the point of overidealizing them) and the hate focuses on the caretakers they are placed with. Because love is more primary and precedes hate and because it is very difficult for a child to reject his parents completely, the split is seldom hate of the natural parents and love of the foster parents.

Unfortunately, what happens to the child from this point on in placement only acts to reinforce this dichotomy of feelings. For example, one feels guilty and disloyal hating and rejecting one's parents. The foster child doesn't have to do this because other people will do it for him. When and if a parent shows up to visit a child in placement, the child doesn't have to be very astute to sense our disapproval of the parent. It is very hard for a foster parent to approve of a drunken mother who comes to visit her child in care, disrupting the home and upsetting the child. Or the child care worker in an institution doesn't approve of the psychotic mother who rambles incoherently during her visit and upsets the child with wild and improbable promises like taking him home for good next week. (Natural parents frequently make promises to take the child in care home to live with them for good, even when they know it is impossible to keep the promises. They don't consciously wish to hurt, deceive, or disappoint the child, but rather their immaturity prevents them from facing the painful reality of their situation.) Add to this that most visiting parents, feeling defensive about being bad parents and having their child placed, tend to come on like parents when they visit. They

make all sorts of carping criticisms about the kind of care
their child is receiving and issue orders as to how their child
should be treated. (It is hard to hear your child call someone else "Mommy.") It is difficult for any substitute caretaker, who after all is human, to put up with such comments
as:

"You've been beating my child. I'm going to sue you"
(from an abusive mother).

"It doesn't look like he's getting enough to eat" (from
a neglectful mother).

"I don't like her dressed in blue. I never liked blue on
her."

"What the hell right have you to cut my child's hair?
I want him to have long hair, not short hair."

"How dare you send my child out of this institution to
visit with a volunteer family for the weekend. If she goes
anywhere, it should be home to me."

"I want a full report of everything bad my child does.
If he gives you any trouble, smack him one right across
the mouth. That's the way I brought him up and that's
what he needs."

Good taste prohibits reprinting the thoughts that leap
to the minds of the foster caretakers in the face of such
provocation. It is enough to say that their attitude toward
the natural parents is less than accepting. The child knows
this and finds himself now free to defend his parents against
the criticism of other people. The anger at the parents is
someone else's, not his, and he can virtuously confine himself to loving and defending his parents.

Then, too, foster parents, child care workers, social
workers, and so on, avoid talking with the child about the
parents. The effect of this silence is to convince the child
that something must be very wrong with the parents if no
one can talk about them. If adults can't bear to mention
them, how can he or she be expected to talk about parents?
There are many reasons why adults don't talk with foster
children about their parents.

- untrained people don't know what would be helpful to say to the child and keep quiet for fear they will say the wrong thing and upset or harm the child.
- busy caseworkers don't have the time to talk with the child.
- sometimes we are embarrassed or ashamed to talk with a child about the unpleasant things parents have done (that they are drug addicts, murderers, child molesters, homosexual, violent and abusive, psychotic, promiscuous, et cetera). We each have our own particular horror that it is hard for us to talk about with children.
- sometimes we feel if we open Pandora's box, the children will express their anger and resentment of their parents, and we wonder if it is desirable to let children express hatred and disappointment and criticize parents (and ultimately the authority that they represent).
- there are some people who, lacking knowledge, believe that if the child doesn't bring the subject of his parents up, then it can't be bothering him or he isn't thinking about it. "Out of sight, out of mind" is their motto; he has forgotten his parents, so why open up old wounds?
- then we all have times when we don't want our own pain increased. When we think of what parents do to children, of all the misery in the world, of the filth, sordidness, and unhappiness — well, some days it is just more than we can bear. (What ever happened to the days when innocence shone like the sun and the rain clouds never came beyond the horizon?)

The more the child expresses his love for the missing parents, and his desire to be with them, the more some of us shudder. We know what the parents are like and we fear the child's love for them. We know that what we love is often what we become and we fear that in spite of all we've done for the child, he may be, in the last analysis, his parents' son or daughter.

A two-year-old throws a temper tantrum (normal for the age) and we recall that his record says his father is in prison for assault with intent to kill. Do you suppose he's developing a temper just like his father's?

A teen-age girl goes boy-crazy (also normal for the age) but her mother was a whore. Isn't it too bad that she is following in mother's footsteps?

There is nothing unusual or abnormal about a child loving his parents. Most children do love their parents. It is abnormal not to love them. Loving the parents is not the same thing as wanting to become like them. True, we are familiar with this kind of positive identification where one wants to become like the person he loves and respects. But this only takes place when there has been a prior positive and satisfying relationship with that person.

What we fear is the child wanting to become like the "bad" parts of the parents. We keep a jaundiced eye on the child to see if any of the parents' bad traits are leaking through. We never tell these children that they have pretty blue eyes like their mother, or her wavy hair, or their father's nice smile. We don't tell them because often we don't see these parents as having any desirable characteristics. We also don't tell them because even if we did see good things about the parents, we are afraid that if we encourage the child's identification with those positive qualities, he will also identify with the negative aspects of the parents. We see bad traits as much more highly contagious than good traits. While we don't want to see these children repeat their parents' past, by denying them the right to love their parents we nudge them to become just like their parents. There is a negative form of identification, too, in which one becomes like someone in order to possess that of which he has been deprived. For some foster children, the only way left for them to be reunited with mother or father is to take the parent inside of themselves, to become like the lost parent.

With the onset of adolescence, the normal drive to be independent of adult control, to be free and your own boss, to be somebody, impels the adolescent into action. Resentment at the caretakers to whom he does not belong wells up. "I don't have to do what you say – you're not my parents."

Rebellion against parental authority is part of adolescence, since growth to adulthood means breaking away from infantile dependence upon the parents. How can you rebel against a shadow? One has to rebel against substance and the foster caretakers become the focus of the resentment that should be directed against the natural parents. To the foster caretakers, it seems like all they've done for the child was wasted, as now he turns against them. But that's the way natural parents also often feel when their children reach adolescence.

The one thing the foster caretakers are likely not to have given the child was a chance to talk about his parents, to understand them and their actions, to keep alive their images in his mind as people who were never able to satisfy his longing to be loved. Instead of turning his longing toward the foster caretakers, there is resentment and hatred, and an argument follows. The child runs away from care, straight to her alcoholic mother at home. She returns to care later that night – staggering drunk – just like a grown-up.

"Just like her alcoholic mother," the staff say, and now it may be true, because it is too late. The parents of the past have reclaimed another child because we provided the child with the illusion of caring; we cared for the body but not for the mind.

Most foster children cannot identify with adequate adult models that they see around them because they have not let go of their parents. Until these children can relinquish the past, they cannot take from the present or the future. This does not in any way mean that children must be helped to "forget" their parents. On the contrary, they must be helped to remember, know, and ultimately to accept their parents as they were. They must be helped to a new and different love toward their parents, not one which rose out of unfulfilled need and deprivation, but one which expresses compassion and acceptance. This partly means they must come to see the parents as unable to care for them, not as unloving or unwanting; and their own placement as a sign that they were worthwhile, not that they were worthless. As with all of us, only when we have been freed from the wish that our parents had been other than they were, will we be able to accept them as they were and to see our life from now on as our own responsibility. If we do not let go of the past, then what we love is what we yet shall be.

These are not easy changes to bring about in the foster child — they do not come quickly, easily, or cheaply; they do not come without concerted effort on the part of caring adults. There is no question that they must come about. If they do not, all the money we have spent on maintenance of children in foster care has been largely wasted. The little we saved by not attending to the child's mental health while he was in care will be spent many times over in the future costs of his psychiatric hospitalization, prison incarceration, welfare payments, unemployment compensation, and, ultimately, child welfare services for his own children.

We need the personnel, time, money, and commitment to prophylactic and rehabilitative mental health services for all foster children, to help them understand why they are in placement and to accept their parents as they are. We know lack of knowledge leads the child to distortions, daydreaming, despair, bitterness, and anger, reinforcing and maintaining his poor concept of his own worth, competency, and sense of who he is. If we don't provide this help, the child will grow up to be a dependent, inadequate, unfulfilled adult.

We deprive the child of his parents in order to save him but do we also mean then to ignore him and deprive him of his chance to grow up to be a healthy adult? We know what the child needs. The only question left is: do we care enough to see that he gets it?

4

What Will Happen to Me?

"Sometimes I wonder why the state won't let me live with my brothers and sisters. I wonder if I will ever see my sister again?"

— EIGHT-YEAR-OLD BOY
IN FOSTER CARE

"Sometimes I wonder what will ever happen to me. Will I get married and will I be able to keep my children? Will I be a good mother to my children and a good wife to my husband?"

— TWELVE-YEAR-OLD GIRL
IN PLACEMENT

"She is sad and unhappy. She is crying because her mother left her"
— *ten-year-old boy*

Theoretically, foster care was conceived as a short-term placement, a way station on the road to adoption. In practice, nothing could be further from the truth. Adoption is a realistic possibility for an extremely small number of children removed from their parents. Only 5 percent of all the children in foster care under public auspices in 1963 were receiving adoption services[1] and not all of them will be adopted. The reasons are many.

One set of reasons has to do with laws regarding adoption, which vary from state to state. In some, adoption is possible only after parents have abandoned the child for a specified length of time. If that length of time is, say, five years and the child enters placement when he is three years old (the most likely age to enter placement is under five), by the time he is legally able to be adopted, he is unadoptable because of his age. It is extremely difficult to place any child over four years of age for adoption and the chances of being adopted are greatest if you are under four, a girl, white, pretty, appealing, very docile, above average in intelligence, and have no irremedial physical defects.

In some cases, adoption is impossible without parental consent, and some parents will never consent to adoption. Many people would prefer to have their children placed in an institution than give them up to another family. Not that they ever hope or plan to take them back again, but adoption implies complete parental failure, whereas having a child in an institution implies a temporary inability to care for him. One whose child is institutionalized can maintain the fiction that someday he or she will become an adequate parent. By the time that's likely to happen, the child will be a man and objectively will no longer need parents. His need for parents will be relegated to a psychic reality.

Other legal barriers in some states are laws preventing interracial adoptions, adoptions by parents of a different religion (a child's religion is often defined as that of the natural mother), and one-parent adoptions. There are certainly problems and dangers inherent in each of these and the laws are supposedly there for the best interests of the child. In other cases, all that these laws protect are the prejudices of the community.

Adoption homes are not easy to find. An increasingly large number of women have joined the labor force; many seek professional careers; and there is a trend toward childless marriages by choice. Farm families, which used to be prime foster and adoptive home possibilities, are becoming fewer in number each year as the population becomes increasingly urbanized. Adoption and foster home care never did have a good name — it was all that was left if you couldn't have your own children. You were taking a chance of getting a bad seed, blood being thicker than water and all that. If you took money for either type of care you were looked down upon — why, it was practically the same thing as being on welfare yourself. In spite of recent trends to single-parent adoptive homes, quasi-adoptions, and subsidized adoptions, both adoptive and foster homes remain hard to find for certain children.[2]

There are many children who, under the best of conditions, are extremely hard to place for adoption. Examples are: the physically handicapped; those needing extensive medical care; the mentally retarded; the mildly and severely emotionally disturbed; the teen-ager or any child over five years of age; and so on. Actually it is difficult to maintain most of these children in foster homes, much less adoptive homes. People have very little tolerance for the even slightly deviant behavior of somebody else's child.

If adoption is not likely, then what does happen to these children in foster care? In 1957, the Child Welfare League of America supported a study on a sample of 4,281 children in foster care in the United States. The results were published in a classic book on the neglected and dependent child, *Children in Need of Parents*.[3] At that time, the authors, Maas and Engler, predicted: "Of all the children we studied, better than half of them gave promise of living a major part of their childhood years in foster families and institutions." [4]

At least that was the prediction at the time. Ten years later, in 1967, Maas undertook a follow-up study.[5] He was able to get information on 422 of the 551 children chosen as a sample of the original group. Thirty-five of the children were still in care ten years later! In fact, a third of all the children had been in foster care for ten or more years and more than half of the group (52 percent) had spent six years or longer in foster care. One could hardly call this short-term care.

More recently, Fanshel[6] reported on a five-year longitudinal study of 625 children who entered foster care for the first time in New York City in 1966. At the end of three and one-half years, 46 percent of the children were still in care. In addition, twenty-six of those discharged had returned to care, some several times. Incidentally, of those discharged, only 5 percent were to adoptive homes.

A similar study reported on 144 foster children in foster homes in the Midwest.[7] As a group, their average length of time in placement was just over three years. However, 62 percent had been in placement two or more years; 37 percent for three or more years; and 20 percent for more than five years.

Jeter,[8] in her nationwide survey of children receiving child welfare services from agencies, included in her data the length of time that had elapsed since the reporting agency first opened a case on a child in foster care. Almost a third of this group had received services for six or more years, including 9 percent that had been served for twelve or more years. (Length of time that services were provided is not the same as length of time in foster care — it can be longer, identical with, or conceivably even shorter than the length of time in foster care.)

That more than half of the children in foster care are spending the major part of their childhood away from their families is only part of the story. The rest of it is — nobody planned it that way! These are truly forgotten children, "Children in Limbo" or "Orphans of the Living," as they have been called.[9] According to the Joint Commission on the Mental Health of Children, for two-thirds to three-quarters of the children in foster care there is no specific plan as to whether and under what circumstances they can return home.[10] That statement would not be true in practice, were it not for the use of the word "specific." Take for example, the study by Bryce cited earlier (see note 7).

In that study, Bryce found that return to the natural parents was the casework plan in two-thirds of the cases at the time of the child's placement.[11] For those 89 children who had already been in care for over two years, return to the natural parents was still the plan in two-thirds of the cases. For the 14 others, there was no plan at all. Long-term placement was the specific plan for only 19 of these 89, even though the average length of placement for this group at the time of the study was already four years.

The situation then is this. Foster care is conceptualized as short-term care, a way station either to adoption or eventual return to the parents. The facts are that a negligible number of children are adopted, and well over half of the children end up in long-term care. The social work plan is that any day now they will return to their parents, but "any day" becomes two years, five years, or ten years, and still they wait, for their parents to be rehabilitated.

What happens while they are waiting? One thing that happens is that nothing happens with the parents. In Bryce's study, casework services were being provided for the natural parents of only twenty of the fifty-five children for whom the plan was to return to their natural parents.[12] In Maas's study, 73 percent of the parents of children in long-term care (defined as ten years or more) were receiving little or no agency treatment.[13] The major reason why almost 60 percent of the children were still in foster home placement, according to Bryce, was that the parents had not been rehabilitated! [14]

At the end of Chapter 1, it was pointed out how, in spite of our professed respect for the integrity of family life, we split up families by placing children in foster care, without first exhausting all available resources to hold the family together. Now another paradox must be pointed out. Once the child is placed, "family" becomes a slogan. We cling to the hope of reuniting a child with his family even when this is unrealistic, in cases where there is no real family, where parents have never established a home, where neither parent has positive ties to the child. How else can you ex-

plain a social worker insisting her plan is to return a child
to his parents, when that child has been in a child care
institution for five years, his father is in jail for life for
murder, and his mother is in a state hospital as a chronic
schizophrenic, with a record of seven past hospitalizations?

According to Maas, for over half of the children in long-
term care, the parents were either content with long-term
care for their child or else had no plan at all in mind for
him.[15] Once the child is placed, most parents are content
to let the status quo remain. The agency which placed the
child doesn't push them to make plans either. Neither do
the courts push. The courts aren't involved in the majority
of the cases anyway, because the placements are voluntary.
In many states, you can go to the department of public
welfare and ask them to take over care of your child because
you can no longer care for him properly. You and the
department work out an informal, voluntary arrangement
which either of you can terminate upon forty-eight hours'
written notice.

This trend away from legal commitments to informal arrangements, like many ideas in social welfare, was sensibly
conceived. Its purpose was to make it easy for parents who
were having difficulties to get help in caring for their child,
that being in the best interests of the child. It also had
as a purpose avoiding court action to remove children,
which usually resulted in angry and defiant parents, who
then spurned all efforts of the welfare department social
workers to help them with their problems. By emphasizing
the welfare of the child and trying to avoid parental resis-
tance to help, this trend seemed like a good idea.

In fact, the practice is a nightmare in which the welfare
department finds its hands are tied. They may make plans
for the welfare of the child, but if the parents object and
threaten to remove the child from care, those plans are
often dropped. If the parents make no plans for the child
and let the situation drift on (as they often do), what can
the state do? They can threaten to terminate the care arrangement, but if the parents accept the child back to an

unchanged situation, then the child has lost. If the parents refuse to be bluffed and won't take the child back, how can the state force them to take the child back, when to do so, by placing him with parents who don't want him, would not be in the best interests of the child?

Of course, the state can decide to terminate the voluntary arrangement by taking the case to court, seeking a permanent commitment to its care. This, too, is often a bluff. Frequently, in voluntary cases, there are no clear legal grounds for separating the parents and child or the necessary legal evidence is not available. The legal definition of neglect covers only a small part of the many cases in which parents fail to care for their children adequately. (For a more detailed discussion of neglect as defined by the laws in various states, see Sanford Katz, *When Parents Fail*, Beacon Press, 1971.)

Before the department of welfare goes to court, it will often try to decide if it is likely to win or lose the case. (The decision to go to court often hinges on which judge is likely to hear the case — some are known to be pro-agency; others wouldn't separate a child from his natural mother under any circumstances.) If there is doubt that the state might win, they won't go into court. So everything stays the same, except the parents are now mad at the state welfare worker for threatening legal action and won't let her in the house anymore. The state continues to care for the child, its ability to aid the parents has been compromised, and the parents perpetuate the status quo. In effect, a legal issue has been settled without the legal system ever having been involved.

Should the state go to court, it may lose the case and the child will be returned to its parents. (There is some evidence that in neglect or abuse cases, voluntary placements lead to longer-lasting placements than do court admissions.) If the state should win the case and then custody of the child, then the child may lose, since he now has a slightly better than fifty-fifty chance of ending up in limbo.

The courts and the child welfare agencies talk a different language. This was shown in a study of the disposition of child neglect cases referred to a juvenile court in Los Angeles County. When requesting placement, caseworkers focused on the current and future needs of children and on parental failure to meet these needs. Their psychodynamically based predictions of adverse future emotional development of children, inferred from parental character problems and inadequacies, were inversely related to court decisions for placement. On the other hand, the courts focused on legally admissible evidence of neglect and were most impressed with clear and present dangers to the safety and well-being of children. When such evidence was presented, placement was usually sustained.[16]

When a child who has been placed enters limbo, this is a state of mind, not a place. It can't be a place, because too often the place where the child stays keeps changing. Bryce,[17] for example, found that the average number of moves for children in placement was 2.7. Some 44 percent of the group had not been moved after the initial placement and 73 percent had moved no more than twice. Quite comparable figures are reported by Jeter in her survey of public agencies in the United States.[18] This still means that over one-quarter of the children (28 percent) had been moved three or more times.

Since foster care was intended to be short-term, transitional care, it was not deemed desirable for the child and foster parents to become too emotionally attached to each other. Many agencies had rules forbidding foster parents from becoming adoptive parents to the children for whom they cared. Foster parents were asked to do a difficult if not impossible job — include the child in a warm, loving, supportive family for an unknown period of time without becoming attached to him. Accumulated research was beginning to point to the disastrous effects on a child's emotional development of being separated from adults (both natural and substitute parents) to whom he was emotionally attached.

When children in foster family care remained too long with one family, they ran this risk of emotional injury when eventually removed. Incredibly, a few agencies adopted an absolutely horrible solution to the problem. Whenever a child showed signs of becoming attached to foster parents, he was moved to a new home. That way, so the reasoning went, he could never suffer the loss of something he was not allowed to develop. The flaw in this incredible perversion of a research finding was that not allowing a child to put down emotional roots turned out to be emotionally even more damaging than pulling up the roots. Children who have had multiple placements become extremely insecure, emotionally flat, develop severe problems in their ability to form relationships with others, and often show other signs of marked emotional disturbance.

Fortunately, this practice never became widely accepted by child welfare agencies, though you can still run across a misguided adherent of the policy. Children still continue to experience multiple placements (one extreme case had twenty-two placements), but not because it's planned that way for the supposed welfare of the child. The reason for moving a child now is because the foster home placement collapses. This occurs for a number of reasons, most of which could be remedied. Some of the reasons are:

- extremely poor recruitment and selection of foster families. Believe it or not, there are some foster parents that turn out to be even more immature and neglecting adults than the natural parents. Foster family homes have been closed because of severe abuse, neglect, and cruelty. Our selection procedures may be poor, but can they be that bad?
- failure of the state welfare department to provide even minimum social work contact and support for foster families. When problems arise with the child, the family that receives no support simply demands that the state remove the child.
- the state welfare department's policy of expediency in

placing emergency care cases in established foster homes, or, because of a shortage of homes, placing additional foster children in an established home. A foster family that might be able to support one foster child adequately now finds itself with two, three, or more to care for, and, receiving no casework support, the home eventually collapses. This kind of Russian roulette played with the lives of children is guaranteed to result eventually in an explosion.

The more homes that a child has failed in (or the state has failed), the more difficult it is to replace the child in a foster family. Eventually the only placement left is institutional care. In recent years, there does appear to have been an increase in the number of children in institutional care who have experienced one or more foster home failures. The more foster home failures a child experiences, the longer he is likely to remain in foster care and the more likely he is to develop serious emotional disturbances.

Among those children discharged rather early in care (within the first year), discharge is apparently related to reason for placement, according to Fanshel.[19] Slightly over half (55 percent) of those admitted because of the physical illness of the child caring person were discharged during the first year of foster care. Roughly 30 percent of those children admitted for the reason of mental illness of the child caring person, or neglect, or abuse, or family problems, were discharged. Only 13 percent of admissions because of the behavior of the child were discharged in the first year. One cannot necessarily assume those discharged were the lucky ones, since there may not have been much of a change in the home situation. Of those discharged, 90 percent went to live either with their parents or with relatives. Over half of them went to mothers without a father in the house.

For those who stayed in foster care, neither the sex of the child, his age upon initial placement, ethnic background or religion, nor mode of entry into care distinguished him from the short-term placements, according to Fanshel. There were some complex interactions among variables that were related to staying in care, but generally Fanshel found his variables accounted for very little of the variance in the discharge phenomena.

Maas found that poverty did distinguish between long- and short-term cases, with 55 percent of long-term cases coming from very poor economic backgrounds versus only 38 percent of the short-term cases.[20] In fact, 75 percent of all the children in foster care in his study came from very poor or barely adequate economic backgrounds, a relationship that will be commented on in a later chapter. Maas also describes the average child in long-term care as a nonwhite Catholic with a below-average IQ. Because of the low intelligence, and a slight but positive tendency of children in long-term care (in his study) to have more physical disabilities, he suggests that they are unwanted because of their imperfections.[21]

It is a jump to reason that since children who have been in placement for over ten years have less than average IQ's, this is a reason for their remaining in placement. Actually, as we now know, the low IQ may be more the result of long-term placement than a cause of it. The religious and racial factors point up the prejudices in our society and probably reflect the regional sampling that Maas used in his study. To be a Catholic in the Southwest, for example, probably also means you are a Mexican-American, a double minority. To be black in Boston means you are also Protestant — twice out of step with the masses in that area. Kadushin,[22] in a survey in Wisconsin, undertaken to find out why children legally released for adoption weren't being adopted, found the major reasons delaying adoption were: race, in 37 percent of the cases; age in 25 percent of the cases; physical and mental handicaps in another 30 percent. It is not unreasonable to suspect that the same factors make it difficult to find adequate foster homes for some children.

Why a child stays in care is a complex issue and probably depends on many interacting factors. The most important of these are probably not related with the child or his family to a great degree. Instead, they most likely reflect characteristics of the social welfare net that the child and his family are caught in. It would include such things as: little or no services to families; lack of funds; too many cases on welfare rolls and too few staff; high turnover of welfare employees; chaotic and inefficient welfare department administration; poorly trained staff; bureaucratic bungling and incompetence (lost records; misplaced files; failure to assign cases; jurisdictional disputes over cases; inadequate supervision [both of workers and families]; incredible red tape; doing what is expedient rather than what is in the child's welfare; et cetera). Much of what is done is in direct violation of child welfare knowledge. Placements are more determined by what facilities are available than they are by the needs of the child.

Almost anyone who works with neglected and dependent children in foster care can provide a similar picture of the children and their families, the foster home crisis, the problems of their own state welfare departments — for they are much the same throughout the country. One of the clearest, most extensive, and shocking records of the problems of children in longer-term foster care is to be found in Eisenberg's article, "The Sins of the Fathers." [23] Based on his experiences as a consultant to the foster care division of a welfare department in Maryland, he documents the price many of these children pay for their years of parental and public neglect. The 140 children in the sample in his study had all been referred for child psychiatric services.

When this sample was compared with foster children who had not been referred, it was found that the referrals were children who had been in care longest and who had been in a larger number of placements. Slightly more than a third had been in care less than three years; almost a quarter from three to five years, and 40 percent for five or more years. More than half of the clinic cases had three or more placements, more than a third had four or more, and at least a fifth had five or more, during their time in care.

"I am mad because Mother screams at me" — five-year-old girl

The reason given most frequently for the many moves was the demands of the foster parents that the child be removed from the house. This occurs because the home received little casework support. Eisenberg describes this as infrequent visits by untrained workers who changed with bewildering frequency because of the rapid turnover of welfare department workers. (The situation is so bad in some departments of welfare that anyone who has two years of service is eligible to become a casework supervisor because of seniority!)

Concerning intelligence, Eisenberg found 15 percent with IQ's below 69, the cutoff point for definite mental defect. Fifty-six percent fell in the range from 70 to 89, the borderline defective to low average range of functioning. About a quarter were between 90 and 99, in the average range, while only 5 percent exceeded an IQ of 100. These data correspond well with those obtained from the school population of a large Massachusetts institution for neglected and dependent children. (Incidentally, corresponding percentages for a normal population for the same categories would be: 2.6 percent; 20 percent; 23 percent; and 54.2 percent.) It is easily seen that the foster child sample is skewed toward the lower end of the range. This is entirely consistent with what is now known about the depression of IQ scores by adverse environmental factors, one form of psuedo-retardation.

Those who work with deprived children in an educational setting, as Eisenberg also shows, and as lowered IQ scores would indicate, find marked academic retardation. In Eisenberg's group, only 10 percent were placed in the appropriate grade in school, with as many as a quarter of the group being three or more grades behind. The academic area of most marked retardation is the reading level. The children are often inarticulate in expressing their thoughts and feelings; are poorly orientated in time, place, and person; apathetic and mistrustful of adults (teachers, child care workers, or psychiatric clinic staff); and often are unsocialized when they come into care. Poor eating habits and table manners are evident and often bowel and bladder training are weakly established.

The diagnoses of the children in Eisenberg's sample showed over half classed as personality disorders or adjustment reactions of childhood. (These are broad diagnostic categories that involve basic failures to develop or to handle the age-appropriate stresses of childhood.) For example, the most common single reason for referral was aggressive behavior (70 percent of the sample). Serious school difficulties were problems for half the group; one-third had episodes of stealing; one-fifth showed deviant sexual behavior; one-sixth had run away repeatedly; and one-tenth had made overt suicide attempts. (This gives some idea why these children are so hard to maintain in foster homes.) There was some evidence to suggest that the incidence of psychiatric problems increased in foster care rather than being alleviated. Bear in mind that this compendium of pathology represents only children referred for help — one can only guess at the reservoir of pathology present in those foster children who don't get psychiatric services. Maas and Engler[24] estimated that 40 to 60 percent of their sample of children in foster care showed symptoms of psychologic disturbance as compared with about 10 percent of the general population. Eisenberg estimates the incidence of referral of children under eighteen to psychiatric clinics at 3 per 1,000, but that for children in foster care as ten times greater, at 30 per 1,000.

Eisenberg asks the question, "Is it not time that we examine the very nature of foster care itself?" A similar sentiment was voiced by Fritz Redl, in a presidential address to the American Orthopsychiatric Association.[25] In considering the amount and degree of psychologic disturbance in children in foster care today, he wondered if we shouldn't get rid of the obsolete slogan that "even for a very disturbed child, after the neighbor's dog, a 'foster mother' is still the child's best friend." He concluded that as an institution for safeguarding the mental health of vulnerable children, the foster home of yesterday is either extinct or not sufficient anymore.

Why this might be so is shown in another study.[26] Part of the study focused on the characteristics of 148 foster mothers and fathers. Their median age was just over fifty; they had cared for an average of eight children over the past ten years; and they currently had an average of three children in their homes. Most of the foster parents were limited to one social class — they were socially and economically underprivileged. Their educational levels and income were minimal. Their attitudes toward the children in their care was most often ambivalent; they frequently lacked empathy for the foster child's situation and often were completely unable to comprehend his needs. In part, this is a reflection of low educational level, but more it is the same problem these children originally encountered with their parents, that is, socially and economically deprived adults cannot give what they never received. How a social agency can place a child in a foster home that is as inadequate as the one from which he has been removed, and consider it in the interests of the child to do so, is puzzling. To place a child in such a home and then not supervise it but once every two months or so (as is the case with many state welfare departments), is definitely not child welfare — it is public child neglect.

These criticisms are not an indictment of foster care as a type of care. The damage to children in foster care is produced by the low quality of that care and the largely unplanned nature of the service. Both of these conditions exist because of the incredible indifference of the public to the fate of thousands of American children. (See the following chapter, "Am I Worth Caring For?")

As long as five years ago, individuals in the child welfare field were calling attention to the dangers of unplanned long-term foster care. Others pointed out that this is a logical outcome of our attitudes of considering foster care an inferior, third-rate alternative to returning to one's own parents or adoption. (Only institutionalization was considered worse, a maligning and unfair opinion, given the excellent quality of many small institutions for group care in this country today.)

Institutions exist and will continue to exist because there is a need for places for children who can't make it in foster homes. One can still see the remains of the century-old argument, discussed in the Appendix, "Which type of care is best?" rather than "Which type of care does this child need?" There are still too many people in the child welfare field who are operating under archaic rosy principles such as, "Every child has a right to grow up in a family that is legally his own," and "Alternative forms of care are neither necessary nor in the child's best interests." An excellent article on the validity of long-term foster care which attempts to develop a rationale for diagnostic indications for that type of care has been published by Kline.[27] There is no one type of care that is the answer to the needs of all children.

Children who stay in placement for more than a year and a half stand a good chance of becoming professional foster children. They are rarely or never visited by their parents, in spite of the fact that children who maintain parental ties adjust better to placement and do not develop as severe problems about identity.[28] The children are trapped by parents who need to maintain the illusion of possession, and by social workers, courts, and a public that will not act to clarify the child's situation because they need to believe in an illusion of family. As already documented, the psychologic consequences to the children are not encouraging. It is no wonder that the child in placement asks in despair, "What will happen to me?"

So far, a short-range answer to that question has been given. There is also a long-range answer, that is, what former foster children are like as adults. In turning to the literature for answers, one finds that virtually nothing has been published on permanent and long-term foster care. According to two authors,[29] between 1950 and 1970 only five studies, totaling less than sixty-five pages,[30] appeared in print on these two types of care. In all, these studies dealt with less than a thousand children, over 90 percent of whom had been placed ten to thirty years ago, under circumstances much different from those prevailing today.

One of the first attempts to evaluate foster care (specifically foster family care) dates back to the last century and the work of Charles Loring Brace, the New York Children's Aid Society's pioneer of "placing-out." According to Wolins,[31] in 1876 the National Prison Congress charged that Brace's children were filling the prisons of the Midwest, especially in Michigan, Illinois, Indiana, and Wisconsin.

Brace ordered his agents to search the prisons, reformatories, insane asylums, and houses of refuge, with particular attention to the first three named states. Soon he was able to report that of the ten thousand children sent to Michigan and Illinois from the streets of New York City, not one boy or girl was to be found in the prisons and reformatories. Brace and his son continued their evaluation over the next twenty-five years, turning in cheery reports of the unparalleled success of his program.

One might wish to question how much of the quality of life is revealed by the fact that a person doesn't end up in a jail or mental hospital. Another study, also mentioned by Wolins, was done almost fifty years after Brace's. It also concerned children in foster family care. Interviews with about five hundred persons over eighteen years of age who had been in foster care as children showed three-quarters to be "managing their affairs," 11 percent as "harmless," and 12 percent as "definitely at odds with society." This still leaves much to be answered about what these children were like as adults.

In the mid-sixties, Meier[32] produced two studies on the current circumstances of former foster children. The studies have limited relevance for today, since they involve children placed during the thirties, in a time of economic depression, in "free" homes in a largely rural environment in Minnesota. The author did find a somewhat higher incidence of marital breakdown, illegitimate births, and miscarriages, stillbirths, and other neonatal deaths in this group than in a general population. There were also many problems concerning this group's "sense of well-being," with a suggestion that foster care had a differential impact on boys and girls.

The radical nature of the shift in the population coming into care can be shown by citing some statistics from a 175-bed child care center in Massachusetts. In the middle 1950's, this institution served 1,300 children a year. The average length of stay was three months. One third of the children were admitted because of physical illness of the mother and another third while mother was having another baby. Ten years later, the institution served 400 children whose average length of stay was slightly over one year. (By 1972 this had jumped to nearly two years.) Illness of the mother still accounted for a third of the admissions, but maternity reasons had dropped to 2 percent; mental illness of the mother as a reason for admission had tripled, and foster home failures now accounted for 10 percent of all the admissions.

In the fifties, this same institution had available occasional consultation services from an attached out-patient community psychiatric clinic for children. Ten years later, the clinic had greatly increased its staff, who now devoted their entire time to in-patient diagnosis, treatment, and consultation services, so great was the need of the children now in care. This is indicative of the tremendous increase in psychiatric problems that the children in residential care are now showing. This is the major characteristic that makes today's foster children so different from those of thirty years ago. Children now come into care because of social disorganization of their families and parental personality disorders that are so severe as to preclude their ability to provide adequate care for their children. The chronic psychosocial disturbances in the parents result in multiple psychologic disturbances in their children. The major area of damage for the children is in their inability to form new relationships. As a result of their past experiences, they are fearful, suspicious, demanding, distrustful, complaining, and defiant of adults. Their behavior is often aggressive, hostile, and hyperactive.

Probably the most telling argument for what ex–foster children are like as adults can be found very simply by going back to Chapter 1 and paying attention to the backgrounds of the parents as given in the five family cases. These cases were selected out of a few hundred to illustrate reasons for placement. Note how often the parents of these children now in care were foster children themselves.

While it is true that these cases are the ones that stand out, it is not possible to say how many other ex–foster children don't end up with their own children in placement. We don't hear about the successes, but then there is very little in the present situation to make us optimistic about

how many there will be. Many of the children who finally
do leave placement after many years end up back with one
or both of their parents, in an essentially unchanged home
situation. Perhaps they are stronger for having been away
from their parents and for a time may have received better
care than they would have at home. To know the outcome
for sure, we will have to wait twenty years. By then it may
become clear without question that we had our chance to
intervene and really help the child and failed to take it.

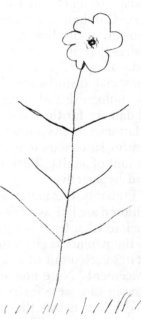

*The small size of the child suggests feelings of
insignificance in this six-year-old girl*

5

Am I Worth Caring For?

"The community would be demoralized by witnessing the expenditure of public money in behalf of the outcast children of shiftless or unfaithful parents." [1]

"What the wisest parent would want for its child, this is what the community should desire for all its children."

— JOHN DEWEY

"Me" by a six-and-a-half-year-old boy in foster care

The child in foster care asks himself the question, "Am I worth caring for?" and answers that he feels he is not, because his parents did not care for him. When the state steps in to take over the caring role for the parents, it often does no better, substituting public neglect for private neglect. It provides only the illusion of caring, for it cannot be caring when the children are still hurting.

In 1959, Maas and Engler wrote *Children in Need of Parents*, and the children are still in need. In 1964, Leontine Young wrote her book *Wednesday's Children*, a study of child abuse and neglect, and the children are still "full of woe." This present book is about society's treatment of one group of neglected and dependent children, those in long-term foster care, or perhaps it should be called "long-term foster neglect," for the children are still hurting.

Society allows too many people to "care" for foster children who are insensitive to the children's needs; who lack even a basic understanding of their feelings; who make decisions affecting the children's lives with little or no professional training, operating instead on good intentions, unquestioned prejudices, and rosy but unexamined myths about families, parents, children, and childhood; who fail to provide rehabilitation services to the parents; and who allow children to sit in limbo for a major part of their childhood without either realistic plans to reunite them with their parents or psychiatric help to aid them to accept their loss.

Certainly no one believes that the poor quality of care these children receive from the state is by conscious design. Some of it may be public ignorance of the situation, lack of funds, lack of trained personnel, indifference, and even incompetence. These things do lead to poor care and services but they are not the ultimate cause of poor care. The children receive indifferent and neglectful care from the state because society does not value them very highly. If society cared enough, if it valued enough, there would be money to train personnel, to build and staff adequate facilities, to provide needed services, and there would be competent people in the state welfare programs to provide leadership and direction to an informed public. The care that the children receive is a reflection of the value that society places on them. For the foster child, society's answer is clear: "We do not value you very highly." How is this possible in a nation which prides itself on being a child-oriented society? America's commitment to its children is largely a myth. It consists of a good deal of rhetoric and very little action, and actions are a much better index of true attitudes than are words.

It would be rather easy to talk about actions that are necessary to improve the quality of care for the foster child. One could cite the need for better selection of foster homes, for changes in our laws regarding these children, for more family support services, and so on. The literature contains many imaginative and innovative programs by both public and private agencies which led to an increase in the number of adoptions,[2] or provided foster home care for children with severe medical problems,[3] of an emergency parent service for neglected/abused children,[4] or a halfway house program to reunite families and children.[5] There are many things that others have done that could be profitably duplicated elsewhere.

But to talk about actions and programs would be largely a waste of time. The problem is not knowing *what* to do; the problem is not being able to *do* those things. We do not act because we are held back by negative attitudes. Before society can undertake positive actions to improve the welfare of the foster child, some of our values and attitudes must change. What are the attitudes which keep us from giving children what we know they need and how must those attitudes change?

The answer to that question is a very complex one. The attitudes in question are a basic part of our way of life and our very concepts of human nature. They are reflected in our government, legal system, methods of child-rearing, family life, and institutions which deal with children. These attitudes are not separate but intertangled. They reinforce (and in some cases contradict) each other. As with a badly knotted ball of string, it is difficult to know where to grab and pull in order to untangle the entire mess. For simplicity's sake, one can focus on the attitudes derived from the two words used to describe these children, namely, "dependent" and "children." The fate of the foster child is entwined with the value America places on all of its children and society's attitudes toward dependency.

Time for Child Power

One reason why neglected and dependent children receive so little attention and such poor care is because they have a low visibility. The chances are good that you neither know a foster child nor can name a person among your acquaintances who is a foster parent. Many people cannot name a local child care agency or an institution that provides care for foster children. Such institutions are usually removed from the mainstream of the community. To the community, the best place for those children who are likely to be a source of corruption to the community is in an institution.

As is true with all those whom we fear and do not understand (the mentally ill, the delinquent, the retarded, et cetera), we hide them away in institutions, which offer proof of service. We rationalize that it is good for children to have the fresh country air, but the high brick walls often built around such places were there to keep the children in and the public out and symbolically said, "We don't want to see what goes on behind these walls." The children are cut off from the very treatment they most need — healing emotional relationships with a concerned community.

Many people still think of these institutions as orphanages, which they are not, and of children in foster family care as orphans, which they are not. Perhaps we would rather believe that they have no parents than face the kinds of parents they do have. The public has lost touch with these children and has no awareness of how the children feel.

An abrupt reminder of this comes at Christmas. Quantities of toys and gifts pour into institutions in the weeks prior to Christmas, donations to brighten Christmas for the children. But the resulting mound of cheer is three-quarters junk. There are dirty, dog-eared books, trucks and tricycles with one wheel off, cuddly toys with the stuffing falling out and the fur matted with old food, games with half the pieces missing, dolls with only one arm and an eye that won't close, four pieces of broken train track and a battered caboose, a half-used chemistry set and six old bingo cards.

Who would wrap a broken toy in bright Christmas paper and give it to a child? What are people thinking? Do they mean to say, "This is worthless to me, so I'll give it to some worthless child?" Perhaps that is too hard on well-meaning people. Once they paid good money for these toys — they were worth something to someone. Now they have no further use for them, but they can't bring themselves to throw it away, so they give it to charity. They have gotten the last ounce of use from it by giving it away, and if others then throw it away, that's their sin. They feel noble but give no thought to how the child who receives the gift will feel. Regardless of the giver's intent, if a child received a broken toy, he would read in the message, "This toy is no good, therefore I am no good, because it was given to me."

Christmas is the one time of the year when children in institutions are highly visible, even if nobody really sees them. As for the rest of the year, well, nobody shows up to give the children a Fourth of July picnic, or a Halloween party, or a birthday party for all of the Scorpios. Christmas is for remembering kids in institutions, but the rest of the year is for forgetting them.

Any group with a low visibility has a public image problem. In this age, if you want to be visible, you have to hire a public relations man to work on your image. Big business has its lobbyists, as do the physicians, farmers, labor unions, and fishermen. But who represents the interests of children to the government? What children need is an advocate, someone to express child power.

For some sixty years, children did have such an advocate. The Children's Bureau[6] crusaded for better child and maternal health, child labor legislation, and universal public education. It also administered some of the child welfare funds under the Social Security Act. In 1972, President Nixon saw fit to disband the Children's Bureau and sprinkle its remains among other government agencies. Whether or not the voice of children has been effectively stifled in Washington remains to be seen. Perhaps the new Office of Child Development can be as effective a spokesman for children as was the old Children's Bureau. Recently the OCD convened a National Action for Foster Children Committee[7] to learn the facts about foster family services in communities, make citizens aware of these facts, and take action to improve the life of foster children. Though just beginning, the goal of NAC is to establish one hundred state, city, or county action committees this year. Another strong advocate for children's welfare for many years has been the Child Welfare League of America,[8] which publishes the journal *Child Welfare*. A private organization which draws its support largely from child welfare professionals, it is not widely known to the public.

The Joint Commission on Mental Health of Children recommended a plan to give children a national voice in government. They suggested a nationwide system of advocates and child development councils.[9] Three years have passed since the report and nothing has been done to accomplish this. If special groups of children, like foster children, are ever to obtain high visibility, there must be a strong national voice to speak out for the interests of *all* children in our country.

While this will do much to set a favorable climate, the real action for children must come on a local level. Every child in trouble, whether a foster child, delinquent, emotionally disturbed, or retarded, should have a personal advocate, someone from his community (such as a minister, businessman, housewife, or service club member) who will take an interest in the child and represent him in all matters. This definitely should not be someone connected with either the courts or a child welfare agency, but someone in addition to these people. Such a person would be a gadfly — to nudge the courts, welfare agencies, social workers, the state, and the institutions to make plans for a particular child and see that they are implemented. Perhaps this is one use we could make of our aged, along the lines of the very successful foster grandparent program that many institutions have. (This excellent program meets the needs of two groups, children and the aged, for each federal tax dollar spent.) For change to occur in children's welfare, our attitudes must shift to the point where those who are not injured become as indignant as those who are.

People, Not Problems

One unique aspect of the problem of visibility is that large numbers of people can very easily be invisible. One would think that we could easily lose sight of a single individual, but could scarcely miss seeing a crowd. In fact, the reverse is more often true — the individual is highly visible, while the group becomes a blur of anonymous faces. We can respond to a starving child on a one-to-one basis, but are overwhelmed by the magnitude of trying to feed a million starving children. The problem is so staggering that we throw up our hands in despair and say, "There is nothing that I can effectively do about this."

In the Appendix, it will be seen that specific services for children grew out of a community's response to a particular local crisis, such as a flood, plague, massacre, or other disaster. On a state or national level, our actions are removed from a personal meaning. On a large scale, the starving child becomes the social problem of poverty. When we focus on social problems, they acquire a reality of their own and human tragedy is depersonalized. Thus we devise programs to attack problems (War on Poverty) rather than to aid people.

America can be very generous when it is personally involved in tragedy. The entire nation can hold its collective breath and pray while the television cameras show us the large-scale efforts mounted to rescue two children buried under tons of sand that shifted treacherously while they were playing on it. Dollars pour in from all over the country to a special fund for the family burned out of their home on Christmas Eve. The individual case gets action, but our hearts are cold and our pocketbooks tightly shut to the invisible crowd.

A six-month-old infant in Boston is removed from his family because he is found to be malnourished — while over twelve million children in the United States under the age of eighteen live in families too poor to feed and house them adequately.[10]

A ten-year-old child in a child care institution, placed there because of his mother's mental illness, receives dental care for his badly rotted teeth — while almost half of the children in America under the age of fifteen have never been to a dentist.[11]

A sexually promiscuous woman with an illegitimate child is on welfare. Her worker helps her obtain contraceptives — while in the rest of the country, one baby in seventeen is born to an unmarried mother, with four chances out of ten that the mother will be between fifteen and nineteen years old.[12] There are a minimum of 800,000 unwanted births in the United States each year (half to the poor or near poor) and over 1,000,000 illegal abortions.[13]

A welfare mother has a worker who arranges for her to get prenatal care during her pregnancy — yet one baby in five in this country (750,000 children) is born to a mother who has received little or no obstetric care.[14] There are twelve countries of the world with infant mortality rates lower than that of the United States.[15]

A Care and Protection complaint is taken out against a mother who leaves her four-year-old girl alone most of the day while she works — but the Child Welfare League of America estimates that 50,000 children under the age of six look after themselves while their mothers work. Over four million children under six have mothers who work, but there are only 613,000 spaces available in day care centers.[16]

A routine screening test picks up an abnormality in an infant which can be easily treated, preventing the development of severe retardation — but of over two million mentally retarded children born each year in the United States (many to poor families), half of the defects could have been prevented if we applied what we already know about medication and treatment before birth.[17]

A child from a middle-class family is receiving psychiatric help from a child guidance clinic for a serious emotional problem — but he is only one of 500,000 who receive such help, a mere 5 to 7 percent of the 1.4 million children in the United States who are acutely in need of psychiatric care but not receiving it.[18]

There is no need to carry these examples further. The few that get help are the ones we see, but are only a small fraction of those who need help. We see, yet we are blind; we hear, yet we are deaf; we feel, yet we are not touched. The foster child is not singled out for poor care — we treat all of the nation's children poorly.

Why Not Children?

"The interests of the nation are involved in the welfare of this army of children no less than in our great material affairs." [19] This statement, from the 1909 report of the first White House Conference on Dependent Children, marked the first time the federal government became even minimally involved with children. Prior to this, child welfare had been the sole responsibility of the states. Though we have still not implemented the recommendations of the 1909 conference, a White House conference on children continues to meet every decade. This is an excessively long interval between reevaluations of the welfare of the children in the nation. Virtually a whole generation of children grows up in ten years. In the past fifty years, the federal government has done much to promote the welfare of children[20] (child labor legislation, Aid to Families with Dependent Children, universal public education, et cetera), but with the exception of the last, it has never been broad in scope or anywhere nearly adequately financed. (As one legislator put it, "We authorize dreams and appropriate peanuts.")

We accept without question that government has a function in regulating business, building a network of roads, stockpiling agricultural surpluses, and paying farmers not to farm (if our welfare system can't bring itself to pay people to help support the children they do have, maybe we could see our way clear to pay them a bonus for every child they agree not to have!), exploring space, thinking about controlling pollution of our environment, financing public education, supporting medical research, developing a supersonic jet and subsidizing faltering aircraft companies, providing for national defense, moving the mails (on second thought, delete that), dealing with foreign governments, saving the world for democracy, collecting taxes, and preserving our national resources.

What we don't see government as doing is directly helping people improve the quality of their lives. Our list of national resources does not extend to include people (with the sole exception of the national labor force). We certainly don't see our children as a national resource. Ask an American what the value of something is and he'll tell you how much he paid for it. This also works in reverse. Know how much Americans pay for something and you can tell how much they value it.

The Aid to Families with Dependent Children program of the federal government (1971 level of spending approximately 3 billion dollars)[21] could be financed:

- for 10 years with one year's expenditures on the war in Vietnam (approximately 30 billion).
- 8 more years by what it cost to go to the moon (24 billion).
- for 4 years by the interest on the national debt (12 billion).
- and for an incredible 25 years by the direct costs of the federal highway program (76 billion).[22]

Children not only receive little of our national income, but their share has actually decreased. In 1950, children received one dollar out of every four that the nation spent on social security and public assistance. By 1965, their share had dropped to one dollar in every six.[23] We see welfare as exerting an increasingly heavy burden on us, yet the ratio of expenditures for public assistance to the total personal incomes of all persons in the United States has remained precisely the same for the last fifteen years.[24] We remain one of the lightest taxed of the industrial nations, collections accounting for about 30 percent of our gross national product (versus 40 to 45 percent in Sweden and Britain).[25]

Socrates once said to the citizens of Athens: "What seek ye fellow citizens that you turn every stone to scrape wealth together, yet take such little heed to your children to whom ye must one day relinquish all?"

For years we have badly allocated our money and resources, favoring special interest groups. Now we find it will cost us staggering amounts to clean up our environment, give us decent public transportation, decent homes in livable cities, better health care and education. Perhaps at last we are approaching the view of government that Jefferson held out to us nearly two hundred years ago — that governments are instituted among men, deriving their just powers from the consent of the governed, for the purpose of securing man's unalienable rights to Life, Liberty, and the pursuit of Happiness. The welfare of children isn't going to improve much until America gets to the point where it can say, "People are our most important product."

Items of Personal Property

A foster child in an institution once asked a child care worker, "Do you know if there is anybody who owns me?" The child was reflecting what is a common view in this country — children are not individuals in their own right, they are items of property, owned by their parents.

Early English common law saw children as items of property.[26] As the loyal subject was subservient to his king, so was the child completely submissive to his father. Even the mother had no legal status, since she, too, bowed to her husband's authority, though she was entitled to reverence and respect from her children by virtue of her role in bearing them. Under English common law, the father had a moral obligation to support, protect, and educate his children. These were not legally enforceable obligations and a father certainly couldn't be held to a standard of either support or education greater than one he could afford. From these fatherly duties came three rights, which could be and were enforced by the courts. They were the right to custody, to punish, and to the services and earnings of a minor child. The first two were important in controlling children, especially the behavior of the firstborn male child, who was the heir. When property was involved, everyone was very attentive to these rights. The third right, to the earnings of a minor child, was especially important if you were poor, for it meant a child could be sent to work to help support the family.

America borrowed much of the English legal system for its own, including the favoritism of property rights over individual rights. Over the years, gradual inroads have been made by the government on the father's absolute authority over his family. For one, the rights of the mother have generally been put on an equal footing with the father's. In some cases, we've done an about-face. An American court held in 1908 that in the matter of the right to determine a child's religious education (part of the right to custody), "the welfare of the infants is best promoted by bringing them up in the faith of their father." [27] In many states now, a child's religion is deemed to be that of his natural mother.

Child labor legislation has limited the right to send the child to work at a young age; universal public education has limited the parents' right to determine a child's education; and child abuse legislation limits the extent to which one can punish one's children. (Even the old English common law held that punishment should be reasonable and not so extreme as to constitute cruelty.)[28]

But these limitations of parental rights have not in any way led to an increase in the rights of children. They still have few if any legal rights, and the few they have are almost always secondary to the rights of the parents. The law seems to assume that children are best raised by their natural parents, as parental love (or maternal instinct) will ensure the child being well cared for. It further assumes that, in the absence of any evidence to the contrary, this must be true. Thus, having philosophized an ideal state of family care, the law assumes it to be the actual state of affairs in all cases which must be specifically refuted in order to establish neglect. This approach may serve to protect the rights of parents, but it doesn't do much to improve the welfare of children. Some judges require an overwhelming amount of evidence before they will separate a child from his natural mother, so strong is the assumption that the child *must* be best off with his mother. This assumption had its origins centuries ago when we knew very little about the emotional needs of children. In fact, it was a time when we hardly recognized the existence of childhood, and after five or six years of age, the child was treated as an adult, albeit one of small stature.

Children do not have the same legal protection that the law gives to adults, even though they are more dependent and helpless and need greater protection than adults. Children can't sue their parents for abuse or maltreatment and children have little protection against assault and battery. It still is not a widespread practice in divorce cases for the child to be represented by legal counsel. Instead the parents' lawyers squabble over the custody of the child. Surely the child's best interests are not identical with those of either one or the other parent. Recent Supreme Court decisions have held that juvenile offenders are entitled to legal counsel in proceedings against them just as adults are. Until recently, it was possible to jail children for indeterminate sentences for relatively minor offenses (stubborn child or runaway) — an unconstitutional procedure if he were an adult — and do it without legal counsel at all.

There is considerable confusion in the case of neglected and dependent children when we separate parental duties from parental rights. Since the rights grow out of the responsibilities, you might think that they would end when the responsibilities were given up, but not so. Children under care of the state who have had no contact with parents for years can have plans to place them in a foster or adoptive home blocked by natural parents who object. It is still difficult to place a child in a foster or adoptive home of a different religion than that of the natural mother.

This seems especially ludicrous in the case of infants, but it comes down to the question of which is more important, to protect the right of the natural mother to have the child raised in the religion of her choice, or that the child be raised by loving and caring adults. The courts frequently respect the rights of the mother over those of the child, since they don't recognize that the child has these rights.

The law, as usual, struggles with precedents from the past, while the world changes radically. Our laws originated at a time when we knew little about children's emotional needs. The law overstresses the fact of biological parenthood, seeing children essentially as the property of their parents. The law does not admit to a modern view of parenthood. Many courts do not recognize emotional neglect and, unless there is attendant physical abuse or neglect, will not act to remove a child from an unhealthy emotional situation.

Much of the push for a positive statement of the rights of children has come not from the law, but from child welfare professionals. Many have suggested that there should be a Bill of Rights for children. The Joint Commission for Mental Health of Children, for example, advocated the following rights be adopted in order to optimize the mental health of our young and to develop our human resources.[29]

1. The right to be wanted.
2. The right to be born healthy.
3. The right to live in a healthy environment.
4. The right to satisfaction of basic needs.
5. The right to continuous, loving care.
6. The right to acquire the intellectual and emotional skills necessary to achieve individual aspirations and to cope effectively in our society.
7. For those who need remedial services, the right to receive care and treatment.

These rights are not so much a subject for legislation as they are an appeal for a commitment from American society to its children. Implicit in such a list is a social revolution — an about-turn for America in the ordering of its priorities. It is a challenge to see children as individuals and not as items of property belonging exclusively to parents.

It calls first of all for a commitment not to special groups such as foster children, the retarded, poor, and handicapped, but to all children. It implies support of all children, perhaps through children's allowances. (America is the only industrialized, Western nation that does not provide children's allowances.) It means improved health services available to all children. The adequate care of children starts with the adequate care of the mother, so prenatal and obstetrical care would also be a goal. It implies decent housing, adequate diets, clean and safe cities to live in, stable parents or alternative forms of caring, and it implies needed services, such as day care, homemaking aid, and treatment facilities for those who need them, within easy reach of their homes.

If we took the Joint Commission's Bill of Rights seriously, our attitudes would have to change. It would mean that at last we realize that until society becomes parents of all children, no child in America is safe.

As the Twig Is Bent . . .

"No child has ever been known since the earliest period of the world, destitute of an evil disposition, however sweet it appears." [30] So wrote a dour New Englander in the last century. The doctrine of infant depravity was widespread and had its roots in religion, being a common belief of most Protestant sects. Because the child's desires were depraved (an outgrowth of a belief in original sin and the inherently evil nature of man), he should never be given what he wanted. To indulge the child was to give in to evil. "Indulgence in infancy makes men monsters in life."

It was the parent's (especially the mother's) responsibility to extract complete obedience and submission from the child as soon as possible by breaking his will. Any defiance of the mother's wishes, that is, the child's expression of his own needs, had to be met by mother's firm establishment of her will as law. When the child grew red in the face, arched its back, and "stiffened its rebellious will," mother had to stand firm, beating the child if necessary, until he crumbled. She knew that this was right for the child's health and safety, to save him from sin and evil.

This may sound harsh, even cruel, to us today. Certainly we are more civilized in our treatment of children and our view of the nature of children. But are we? The attitudes of past generations are amazingly persistent and have more of a hold on us than we realize. Subtly, through our methods of child-rearing and the unverbalized attitudes of parents toward their children, the past can and does influence us. Each generation of parents passes on to their children the attitudes about children that their own parents had. We may consciously reject the *ideas* embodied in the methods of child-rearing of the last century, but the *feelings* attached to those ideas still persist in us.

In consulting with parents and teachers about child-rearing, one frequently hears the question, "But is it all right to let children have what they want?" Parents are concerned with spoiling the child, but behind this lurks the old notion that somehow children's desires are not to be trusted. They wouldn't say "depraved," but perhaps "uncivilized" or "antisocial" are our modern equivalents for this word.

The best evidence for the pervasiveness of our distrust of children and their natural impulses is the school system. One has only to look at the tremendous amount of mindless rules and control that is evident in virtually all schools to appreciate how deeply we distrust and fear what children may want to do. There is great stress on character training, on teaching children virtues like neatness, good work habits, orderliness, honesty, respect for property, and so on. One can almost hear the echoes from the past, "a disregard for the decencies of life is a step toward indifference toward its virtues." Nobody in his right mind would come out against such a sterling list of virtues. The issue is not whether children need these things (they do) but rather whether they need them as much and as often as we think they do, or for the reasons we think they do, or taught to them in the ways we think we teach.

Let a six-year-old tell a lie and you would think the world had come to an end. We must act to stamp out a bad habit before it gets entrenched. We see behavior as persisting — lie as a child, lie as an adult. We see childhood as the only time you ever learn these things — fail to learn honesty as a child and you will never become an honest adult. We have a sense of urgency and crisis about normal behavioral occurrences because we don't see them as normal behavioral occurrences, as steps in a process of learning, but rather as sins, character defects, inherent depravity coming out in the child.

So deeply do we distrust childhood and children that most of us can't wait to rush them off to adulthood.[31] The sooner they outgrow childhood the better. Again the echoes from the past — make the child independent of adults as soon as possible. We rush children away from being selfish, irresponsible, unable to share, jealous, careless, "wasting time," making mistakes, being demanding, acting immaturely, and so forth. We rush children away from the very things it is to be a child. Childhood is a protected time to learn by doing both sterling things and their opposites and observing the consequences. When instead we pressure children to grow up, act their age, get good marks in school, think about their future job, learn the social graces and how to relate to the opposite sex at age eight, we are denying them their childhood. When we use them to satisfy our own needs, desires for social status, and unfulfilled wishes, we treat them as items of property and not as individuals in their own right.

This is an age in which we have seen many minority groups struggle to obtain their civil rights: blacks, women, homosexuals, the American Indian, and others. The largest group still in chains is children. They are denied their birthright — the right to be dependent. Like other minority groups, children also become convenient targets for scapegoating. They are the scapegoats of adults who interpret the behavior of children through their own motivation, or in modern slang, adults put their thing on children.

A father, arrested for beating his child senseless, couldn't remember what it was that the child had done to deserve a beating. It really didn't matter. The father never saw his son's needs. He had his own conflicts around bad behavior, discipline, authority, guilt — he beat his son nearly to death to save his own life.

That is an extreme example, but in less extreme form it is how we raise our children. We do unto them as was done unto us, without any conscious awareness of why we do it. We react from our own conditioned behavior, feelings, attitudes, and values instilled in us as children. We do not understand our children any better than we understand ourselves.

In an atmosphere of religious and moral imperatives, social and psychological imperatives have no place. We are technological geniuses when it comes to the control of our physical world, but we are bumbling idiots when it comes to controlling the inner world. Psychiatry, psychology, child development, learning theory, sociology, and other behavioral sciences have not been widely disseminated, accepted, or understood. If anything, they have been largely misunderstood. There is widespread distrust of child psychology because it is seen as permissive, letting children do whatever they want, giving in to unacceptable impulses. It is as if any approach that seeks to understand the child must be on the side of evil.

We have not come to terms with the destructive forces inside ourselves and we project them onto children. The process is highlighted in the conflict between adults and adolescents, but it is there for smaller children, too. Our reactions to anger, jealousy, greed, self-centeredness, impatience, dependency, irresponsibility, and all else that we see and exaggerate in children call for the dimly remembered responses of generations ago — discipline, force, suppression, authority, lectures, exhortations, and if all else fails, beatings. America wonders where all of the violence in its culture comes from, but it does not see the violence it directs toward children (both physical and psychological). We raise our children in homes and schools in a highly authoritarian manner and then expect that they will understand democracy when they are grown.

We do not care half so much that we understand how children feel as we do that they conform. We concentrate on the outward behavior and not on the emotional impact of our actions. We obsessively read endless books on child psychology to find the latest approved "tricks" to get our children toilet-trained, to clean up their plates, accept responsibility, respect adults, and so on. We believe if we act as parents should, then everything will be all right. *How* we act is not so important as the quality of the doing. Actions may speak louder than words, but they don't speak louder than our attitudes in doing.

In human behavior, as in social behavior, we are willing to look no deeper than the surface. The foster child with the frozen smile on his face must be happy — look, he is smiling. The child, separated from his parents, doesn't ask for them — ergo, he's probably forgotten all about them. It is the appearance that is important to us, not what lies underneath.

So, too, in our approach to social problems. We believe that if only people will act the right way, everything will be all right. We place more stress on form, on visible conformity, than we do on the spirit of the law. More than anything, it is our stereotyped attitudes and prejudices that get in the way of our helping adults and children. With children especially, until we can learn to listen to how they feel, treat them as people, not things, respect their right to be different from us, we will not be able to improve their welfare.

Outcast Children of Shiftless or Unfaithful Parents

The quality of care that we give the neglected and dependent child is perhaps determined more by our attitudes toward his parents than it is by our attitudes toward the child himself. We treat the foster child badly because we disapprove of and do not value his parents. The sins of the fathers (and mothers) are visited upon the next generation. We are not more pro-child because we are too busy being anti-parent.

The first quotation at the beginning of this chapter reflects an attitude from the late nineteenth century that is still with us today. These are the children of shiftless or unfaithful parents, not to mention parents who are lazy, dishonest, promiscuous, alcoholic, immoral, and poor. The primary stigma attached to these children is that they are children of the poor and as such bear the burden of America's belief that to be poor is to be less than a person.

Young's study[32] of three hundred families from private and public welfare agencies (typical of the families in this book) showed: only 10 percent were financially comfortable and able to meet their physical needs. About 40 percent of the families had at one time or another been given public assistance. Only about 20 percent lived in adequate housing. In about 60 percent of the families, the wage earner had not held one job continuously for as long as two years. In nearly three-quarters of the families, the wage-earner was an unskilled laborer. Poor parents also abuse their children and neglect them, as opposed to middle-class families who have "social problems" with their offspring.

What are some of the attitudes we have about the poor and how do they relate to the quality of the care we give their children? At the end of the last century, one of the commonly heard objections to the existence of child care institutions was that they gave parents an opportunity to get rid of their unwanted children, to throw off their most sacred responsibilities. Such a suspicion is not yet dead. Some people still believe that these parents choose not to care for their children. The public reaction, of course, is anger at the parents for attempting to shirk their responsibilities. When we become angry, we act in punitive ways.

Judges deliver morally scathing lectures on responsibilities; social workers use the children to threaten the parents. Perhaps if they take the children away, it will shock the parents enough to motivate them to change their behavior. Or, if the children are already in care, they promise to let them come home for good if the parents will only pull themselves together for the next two months. (As a last resort, you can always suggest you are thinking of foster home placement.)

The trouble with this approach is that you can't force people to act responsibly if they don't have the capacity or don't know how to be responsible. (This is one example of our surface conformity approach — if the parents would stop drinking, all would be fine — never mind the problems that led to the drinking and which will find expression in some other symptom.) The approach rests on the dubious assumption that these parents don't care for their children because they lack the motivation to care. Thus, if you arouse their motivation, they will want to care for their children.

In fact, most of these parents already *want* to care for their children. The trouble is, they *can't*. They were never adequately parented and they cannot parent. They love their children, but they can't care for them. We assume loving and being able to care for are the same thing. They are not. If we focused on the needs of the child, rather than on punishing the parents, we would realize this. It is neither in the interests of a child, its parents, nor society, to exert pressure on any parents to take back or keep a child they cannot care for. We may force them to conform to our ideas of family, but we will have destroyed a child psychologically in the process. If we could find a way to care for their child while giving his parents the love they need, we might just accomplish miracles.

Another prevalent attitude we have toward these parents is that they are promiscuous. While some are (as are some of us), we believe that many of their children are illegitimate. We cannot bring ourselves to use public money to support such people or their offspring. Our Puritan souls (to whom sympathetic understanding is a mystery) rebel at the thought that we might be subsidizing sexual misbehavior if we gave these parents money to support their children. It is a fact, however, that only 21 percent of all illegitimate children in the United States receive support under Aid to Families with Dependent Children and only 30 percent of all AFDC children are illegitimate.[33] A recent study (1969) by Feagin surveyed a selected sample of over one thousand adults on their attitudes toward welfare and AFDC. Sixty-one percent of the sample agreed with the statement: "Many women getting welfare money are having illegitimate babies to increase the money they get." Feagin also reports a recent study in Utah which showed that 90 percent of the illegitimate children on welfare had been born *before* their families went on relief.[34]

It is true that AFDC families tend to be larger than the average U.S. family,[35] which helps contribute to their poverty. Some people also believe that even if the babies are legitimate, the reason for having them is still to increase a family's welfare grant. It is hard to see how the extra $1.50 a day would be worth the cost and trouble of having another child around. Facts, however, have little effect upon people with deeply ingrained attitudes and beliefs.

Nowhere is this more apparent than when we come to the basic reason why we disapprove of these parents. They are poor, which in America means that it is their own fault. In 1823, in New York State, a commission set out to investigate the causes of pauperism. They concluded that the major reasons were:[36]

1. ignorance (either inherent dullness or want of opportunities for improvement, common among the foreign poor)
2. idleness (there was an inherent tendency to this evil)
3. intemperance in drinking (this evil, in relation to poverty and vice, may be called the Cause of Causes)
4. want of economy

(No explanation was given for this last reason — evidently it is apparent. People are poor because they don't save their money, though, since they are poor, it is hard to see how they could have had any in the first place. Nonetheless, the commission straight-facedly recommended the establishment in poor neighborhoods of banks to encourage thrift.)

Of course, all of this was a hundred and fifty years ago and we don't believe that now. Feagin, in the study referred to earlier, asked his sample what the causes of poverty were in America. His results, in order of frequency of responses, were:[37]

1. lack of thrift and proper money management by the poor
2. lack of effort by the poor themselves
3. lack of ability and talent among the poor people
4. loose morals and drunkenness

It doesn't take much retranslation to get: want of economy, idleness, ignorance, and intemperance in drinking!

Poor relief in America, borrowing from England, tried to distinguish between the worthy poor (whose dependent condition could be traced to infirmity, disease, or other disabling cause) and the unworthy poor (who prefer beggary, without labor, to independence supported by industry). The citizens of New York State in the early 1800's were very upset by the increase in welfare costs (pauperism seemed to increase as more money was applied to its relief, giving rise to the view that the solution was causing the problem!) and they railed against "the increase in pauperism, at the expense to the honest and industrious portions of this community." [38]

In 1972, President Nixon said in a speech: "The nation . . . rightly scorns the free-loader who voluntarily opts to be a ward of the state." [39] And Senator Russell Long, chairman of the Senate committee handling welfare legislation, is quoted as saying: "One of the problems we've had with this welfare program is where a mother does not work, does not seek work, and has no interest in justifying her pay from society. . . . There is no doubt that we will fight that battle again this year, of whether people are going to provide money to pay people to be worthless, to be useless, to be of no account." [40] (By the way, note in this that mother staying home and caring for her children is not "work." No one would dare tell a middle-class mother that. But welfare mothers must be willing to work in order to receive welfare. Two values, the importance of mothers to children, and the importance of work for those on welfare, meet head on — motherhood loses!)

We haven't changed much in 150 years in our attitudes toward welfare. The tragic thing is that "there is a towering ignorance in our nation's information centers of the facts upon which intelligent social policy can be based." [41] Our welfare programs (such as WIN) are firmly based on myths. One of the most enduring myths is that welfare rolls are filled with people who "voluntarily opt to be a ward of the state." Feagin's study found 84 percent of the sample agreeing with the statement: "There are too many people receiving welfare money who should be working." The facts do not support this and although they are repeatedly published, they do not have much effect upon beliefs.

In Massachusetts, in 1969, there were about 286,000 people receiving some form of public assistance. A very generous estimate showed only 12 percent were potentially employable. Over half of those on support were children in AFDC households or under the Division of Child Guardianship. A quarter more were elderly, blind, or permanently disabled. Thus, three-quarters of the group were either too young, too old, or too handicapped to work. Of the 20,000 people on general relief, three-quarters were unemployable because of alcoholism, addiction, and physical and psychiatric disorders. [42] James reports on a welfare supervisor in a Massachusetts town who combed the relief rolls for men to help clean the city streets in the spring. Of the two hundred men and women on the rolls, only two men could work, and they were "just about capable of following instructions to sweep the streets." [43] The actual entire work force on the U.S. welfare rolls is estimated to be 50,000 men — less than a tenth of 1 percent of the total welfare population.[44] Yet, a survey of middle-class white Americans, conducted for *Newsweek* by Gallup Poll, found nearly four out of five of those surveyed thought that "half or more of the nation's welfare recipients — erroneously thought to be mainly Negroes — could earn their own way if they tried." [45] Yet we go on designing programs whose major emphasis is to get the loafers back to work. How well will such a program meet the needs of the other 88 percent on welfare?

We are still fighting the myth of the worthy versus the unworthy poor. This is translated into concrete action. For example, in 1965, the average payments per month in Massachusetts were:[46]

Medical care for the aged	$181
Disabled	$152
O.A.A. (old age)	$93
Dependent children	$48
General relief	$37

Clearly here is a table of value, from worthy to unworthy. Nearly five times as much money per month is available for medical care for the aged than for those on general relief. Dependent children are only slightly better off than those on general relief.

A recent Harris Survey, asking people to give their priorities for America's spending, found that 62 percent favored increased spending to help the poor, but that 69 percent opposed increased spending for people on welfare. Said the survey: "Presumably the public feels that simply doling out money to welfare recipients is non-productive, while programs to assist the poor to help themselves are worth spending tax dollars on." [47] Translated into plain English, "helping the poor to help themselves" means getting them back to work. To put it mildly, welfare has a bad name.

A Just and Inflexible Law

Basically, then, the poor of America are seen as being poor because of their own fault. The reasons people give for poverty all point to individual failings of the poor themselves. There are some direct consequences of these beliefs. One is that we never give enough money to welfare recipients to live on decently. This follows the old English principle that the amount of welfare paid should be less than the lowest wage paid to an unskilled laborer in the community. This will force people to work rather than be a burden to the community; if the payments were higher, then people would stop working and become dependent on the government, losing their ambition and motivation. Interestingly enough, England's early adventure into the subsistence allowance, the Speenhamland Act of 1795,[48] tying the level of aid to the price of bread, failed miserably — not because of the loss of motivation of the working man, but because of the greed of the early manufacturers, who promptly cut their wages below the subsistence level, knowing the public would have to make up the difference.

Because we see the poor as responsible for their own poverty, we are angry at them for asking us to give them something for nothing. When angry, we become punitive. One Northern state seriously recommended that after a certain period of time, children in assistance families be removed from the home and placed in government-run institutions. Another suggestion was that mothers be sterilized after their second illegitimate baby.[49] We are angry at these people who break conventions, who offend our moral sensibilities.[50] We would not dream of making such a suggestion of a legally married couple who have ten children, but who work steadily at low-paying jobs.

How much we disapprove of these parents can be seen from the support we are willing to pay for the care of their children. To keep the family intact and the children at home, AFDC pays about $1.50 per child per day. If the children are removed from the home and placed in a foster family, we pay $3 to $5 a day per child. In a child care institution, per diem costs can run $10 to $20. Even further from home, in a residential treatment center, costs range from $25 to $40 a day. Payments for a single child as high as $20,000 a year have been made. The further we get the child from his parents, the more money we pay for his care. (But not always willingly, however. One state legislator, when he found out it costs $5,000 a year to keep a foster child in an institution for neglected and dependent children, exploded: "For that I could send my son to Harvard for a year. But he won't go to Harvard, because I can't afford that for my own children. Why should I pay that for the kid of some drunken bum?") We can hear the echo from the last century: "By a just and inflexible law of Providence, misery is ordained to be the companion and the punishment of vice."

We don't help the children of the poor (and foster children) more because we disapprove of their parents. Our attitude is: "We will help only those children whose parents are of good moral character and willing to work" — just like the position of the charitable organizations of the last century. To help children, our attitudes must change to: "We will guarantee all American children the right to a healthy childhood, regardless of what his parents are like."

Many years ago, child welfare came to the principle that no child should ever have to be separated from his family for reason of poverty alone. Yet poverty remains implicated in the disintegration of the family of the neglected and dependent child. The parents' lack of employable skills, of education, and of healthy personalities doom the family to a borderline existence that drives them to seek escapes in alcohol, sex, marital breakups, and even mental illness. We don't have to approve of the parents of the neglected and dependent child, but somewhere America should be able to find enough compassion to give them the help they need.

The Ultimate Instrument of Public Conscience

The attitude that a man is responsible for his own (and his children's) poverty influences our entire approach to welfare. We essentially see our social welfare programs as residual services, to help a few individuals who have been unable to make use of our other institutions and have fallen by the wayside because of old age, illness, handicap, or misfortune. We assume that able, competent, normal, hard-working, and moral people manage alone and do not need assistance and welfare services. The balance of our programs is begrudgingly given to the lazy, immoral, and incompetent people who we believe choose to live fraudulently on the public bounty. (Yet the poor are not few in number as we believe — the poor of America, if they constituted a separate nation, would rank fifteenth in population among the nations of the world.)[51] For them we have inadequate welfare budgets, low levels of assistance, degradation and humiliation in the delivery of services, invasion of privacy, and deprivation of basic rights — all because we will not accept that living in a complex society may be more than some people can manage and that the demands of family life and raising children are beyond the capabilities of many.

Because of what we assume to be the nature of people who accept welfare, our programs are last resorts, temporary in nature, put great stress upon eligibility, and aim to get people off welfare as soon as possible. Public welfare is where we come face to face with all the other failures of our social institutions. It is itself a monumental failure, a vast conspiracy to turn today's problems into tomorrow's crises. We do not respond to needs — we defer them. Public assistance fails to reach two-thirds of the poor at all, and five out of six of those it does reach are still poor after receiving assistance.[52]

Our view needs to shift to welfare as an institutional part of our society. The concept of government must shift from an emergency repair service to one of active prevention.[53] As a nation, we are sensitive to government intrusion into individual rights or family domain. Perhaps this is because our government was created in rebellion against what we considered arbitrary and unjust exercises of governmental functions. We view government negatively. We see it opposed to individual rights, not as something we the people have created to promote the individual's welfare. We can no longer afford to wait until situations have gone to extremes before government steps in. We need earlier, positive governmental actions that will improve the quality of life for all citizens. We must stop stressing rehabilitation and start stressing prevention. In the face of the many disintegrative and negative influences of modern life, the state has a strong interest in maintaining family life and protecting the welfare of children who will be its citizens of tomorrow.

"The Hate Monster" — nine-year-old boy

Education for Living

Schools, by virtue of the large amount of time they care for children, are one of the great forces acting on children. If they are to improve the welfare of children, schools must become more humane places. Schools must become places where children and childhood are valued, where more emphasis is placed on caring for the child as a person and less on his mind as a separate entity. Schools can build egos, develop self-worth, increase feelings of competency, and, to some extent, temper adverse family experiences. We will need to recruit and train a different caliber of teacher and then pay them more. Teacher education must be overhauled to include much more of the social sciences, both content and techniques. Child development, learning theories, and the nature of childhood would be stressed. Part of the field placement would be in child care areas unconnected with teaching, so teachers can see what non-school behavior is like.

In schools themselves, the curriculum emphasis must shift to teaching skills of living, the major subject being the child himself. We need to explore and learn the skills of getting along with each other, conflict resolution, decision-making, how to value, how to evaluate, when to cooperate and when to compete, and an awareness of social problems and the practical techniques of social action. These things will not be "taught" in the sense of classroom instruction; they will be lived.

A specific need is to include education for parenthood in the schools. This goes far beyond sex education to understanding the impact of critical events that children will face as adults — marriage, birth of children, money conflicts, aging, death of parents, use of leisure time, and so on. These things can be taught in age-appropriate ways made meaningful to the child. Child development and human behavior content are sorely needed. We can no longer afford to be ignorant of ourselves and others.

Education for parenting could be made a prerequisite for obtaining a license to marry, as driver education is becoming increasingly used to obtain a license to operate a motor vehicle. In fact, we are much more strict in making sure people are fit to drive a car than we are in helping them be qualified for the infinitely more complex task of being parents.

The Legal System

Our written laws do have some effect on our attitudes — at least they make explicit a standard for behavior. A most desperately needed change is legislation against the use of violence in children's institutions, from juvenile detention centers to schools and child care institutions. While laws will not stop violence against children, they will at least establish a climate of opinion that renounces the cultural sanctions of violence as a way of rearing and caring for children.

As a second step, there should be an adoption of a Bill of Rights for Children. This is more administrative than legal, but departments of welfare, children's agencies, and government agencies that deal with children should adopt and publicize their formal commitment to a Bill of Rights as a guideline for their actions and policies.

There is a need for a review of our laws regarding the care of children, their welfare, and the conditions for their removal from parents. We can no longer tolerate widely different state laws relating to the welfare of children. Such a review might be a task for a nationwide conference of legal experts, social scientists, and child welfare specialists. The social sciences need to be integrated more into the actual functioning of the legal system. We need to clarify what are the essential legal decisions that have to be made, and which things are best dealt with by extralegal sources. The law is not the best avenue for dealing with social problems.

Federal Government Involvement

High on the list of priorities for the welfare of children is a nationwide health care and possibly allowance system for *all* children. This would sidestep much of the bureaucratic administration, all of the costly investigation of eligibility, and clearly say that all of the nation's children are the concern of society. Giving aid to every child avoids stigmatizing selected groups of children. It is always possible to recoup the aid from those who don't need it through the income tax structure.

Another suggestion is that the federal government commit money to a training program (as they have done for psychiatrists, physicians, psychologists, social workers, public health nurses, et cetera) for a new professional group known as child life specialists. These people would be trained to care and work with children. They would become the future staff of child care centers, consultants or program developers in public schools, professional foster parents, supervisors of child care workers in children's institutions, or house parents in group foster homes.

Child caring professions need improved social respectability, better salaries, and greater community support. The foster home of yesterday is obsolete — in many cases it cannot support even mildly disturbed children. We need to train people whose lifework will be to care for children and work with their families to improve child care. Those who care for children unable to be with their families will not be parent substitutes — they will provide alternative forms of care. For too long we have operated on the assumption that you can replace natural parents. In most cases, you cannot. We have failed to appreciate the meaning of natural parents to a child. We must help the child accept the loss of the natural parents as caretakers, while helping him maintain contact with them when possible, however bad we may judge them to be, and work to facilitate his acceptance of alternative care.

One value of the child life specialist lies in providing a better quality of care while potentially reducing the cost of that care. For example, a child care institution now cares for four children from one family that has fallen apart. At $5,000 to $6,000 per child, that is a yearly investment of

$24,000 in one family. For that amount of money, the welfare department could buy a house, hire a married couple who were child life specialists at $10,000 a year (plus rent-free housing), and move the children into the home with the couple to live as a family. For a few more thousands of dollars for mortgage, living expenses, and mental health consultation, they would end up saving money while providing better care.

Another worthwhile project is for the government to support children's hotels. These might be a combination day care center and short-term care center for children while parents went on a vacation by themselves. Such facilities would be a way of strengthening families by relieving parents of the exclusive care of children and giving them time to cultivate their marriage with each other. Denmark is one country that has such state-run children's hotels.

The Public Media

Radio, television, magazines, and newspapers can function as advocates for children in the community and nationwide. Through articles and documentaries on children's problems and on the institutions and agencies which serve children and their families, they can be both a public information service and a constructive force for mobilizing the public to care for all of its children.

The Public Itself

Community action and service groups can make children an object of their attention. They might join an agency like National Action for Foster Children. They, too, could serve individually as advocates for specific children in trouble, as was suggested in the last chapter. On community, state, and national levels, we would do well to have private groups that serve as advocates for improving the quality of life for all citizens. (These groups might be similar to the consumer protection groups now springing up over the country.) These human welfare councils could think about, evaluate, advocate, and challenge us to improve the welfare of all citizens. These groups could function as a social conscience to remind us that it is people who have problems.

In concluding his discussion on public intrusion into the parent-child relationship, Katz said in his book, *When Parents Fail*, that "it should be remembered that intervention is an intrusion into the privacy of the family, and hence in itself undesirable." Intervention doesn't always have to be intrusion nor does it have to be undesirable. How far can society allow parents to go in raising children exactly as the parents see fit? (To test your feelings on that matter, ask yourself the question, "Do parents have a right to bring a child up to hate or to be prejudiced?") At some point, parental rights must conflict in some cases with the rights of society. Eventually, parents who do a poor job inflict their children on society.

While we do need safeguards on government's ability to intrude into the lives of citizens, if government acted before problems reached a crisis state, if government took on a role of "welfare" facilitating, if it put major efforts into creating the conditions that would strengthen both individual and family life, if it helped us cope better with the stresses and strains of our society, perhaps then there would be *less* need for government to intervene directly into family life.

For changes like that to come about, many of our attitudes will have to change, including our ideas about the role of government in the lives of people. Those changes will occur when Americans are able to couple understanding with caring.

Appendix

A Brief History of Foster Care

"The progress of a state may be measured by the extent to which it safeguards the rights of its children."

— GRACE ABBOTT[1]

"One of the indices of the progress of a society toward the promotion of human dignity is its care and treatment of all children in all social strata."

— SANFORD KATZ[2]

"This girl is sad because her Mommy didn't come to her birthday party"
— *seven-year-old girl*

It wasn't long after the early settlers came to America that they encountered problems in child welfare. Life in the New World was cruel and hard. The virgin forests had to be cleared for crops and houses and defended against hostile Indians. Especially in New England, the climate was harsh and in the early years starvation was never far removed. Medical care was virtually nonexistent and even when available, medical knowledge was primitive. No wonder that the average life expectancy at birth was only a little more than thirty-five years.

137

Life was difficult for an adult but it must have been even harder for children. If you survived the first year of life, the chances were great that you might be deprived of parents through deaths from accidents, Indian massacres, childbirth, illness, epidemics of yellow fever or cholera or war, not to mention alcoholism, poverty, abuse, desertion, mental illness, and neglect. No one knows how many children were left to fend for themselves in the early days of the settlement of America.

The mother country of England didn't help the natural orphan child problem in the colonies by its practice of scouring the streets of English cities for homeless children and shipping them off to America. In 1619–1620, the Virginia Company of London recruited in the almshouses and among the poor of London children to strengthen and increase its settlement in the New World. A hundred children over twelve years of age were sent the first year, but a number died on that long and difficult trip. In 1627, ships left England with fifteen hundred children, bound for Virginia.[3] The company saw in the children a source of cheap labor, while England saw a way of ridding itself of dependents who otherwise would be a burden on the local parishes.[4] They passed their burden on to the colonies.

The colonists had their own problems settling in the New World and weren't about to come up with creative solutions to the social problem of dependent children. Instead, they quite naturally turned to their experiences with the customs of their homeland for ready-made answers. They borrowed the English approaches to the problem of caring for dependent children and transplanted these methods onto American soil.

English Child Care and Poor Relief[5]

The care of dependent children is intimately intertwined in English history with the problem of the poor. When we speak of the English experiences, we are talking about caring for poor children. At first, children were not treated differently from poor adults. It took hundreds of years for the needs and welfare of children to be separated from those of adults, and we still have not managed it completely.

While it is not surprising that early American patterns of child care were borrowed from England, it is surprising that the English heritage of child care had its own historical roots buried deep in the Middle Ages. One can trace the practices and attitudes of this not very enlightened period of world history to the seventeenth century in England, jump to the colonies, and continue to present-day America. Much of our contemporary thinking and practice in both child care and treatment of the poor is firmly rooted in the Middle Ages, literally.

The Middle Ages to Elizabeth I

Life in the Middle Ages, that period of time from the fall of the Roman Empire around A.D. 400 to approximately the 1300's, was unique in social organization. The dominant economic, political, and social way of life was feudalism. The monarchy was weak and power was in the hands of the landed nobility. The life of the poorer segment of the population was organized around the manor. The peasants were not mobile but lived under bondage to the lord of the manor. The old, the sick, and dependent children were cared for as a common family. Each worked to the extent of his ability and was cared for by the manor, so that there was little need for public or private charity.

The dominant institution in England during this period was the Roman Catholic Church, wealthy, landed, and very much involved in the religious, political, social, and economic life of the country. The monarchy was in no position to oppose the Church's execution of what we would now consider secular or governmental functions.

From early times, the Church preached the doctrine of Christian responsibility for its own poor. At first, the Church tried to prevent pauperism, but gradually there grew up the doctrine of the religious merits of poverty. Almsgiving became a pious act, an outward reflection of inner grace, a road to salvation for the charitable. To give alms to the poor, nurse the sick, feed the hungry, aid widows and small children became a religious duty, done not so much to help one's fellow man, but to save the soul of the donor. Eventually, religious orders grew up, dedicated to a vow of poverty. Those who gave away all worldly possessions and relied upon the charity of the godly were people of superior sanctity. The Church's religious sanction of begging brought it eventually into sharp conflict with the government, which saw beggars as a nuisance, a threat to their power to keep the peasants on the farms and a scourge upon the countryside.

Through most of the Middle Ages the Church became the major agency for the relief of those poor not cared for under the manorial system. The practice developed among the wealthy of giving a yearly tithe to support the Church and a third of this money was channeled into poor relief in the local parish. Sometimes money payments were made to widows to care for their own or other's children. This latter arrangement was a form of "outdoor relief" (or relief given in the home) and was an early forerunner of the foster home plan.

The major form of the Church's ministry to the poor soon became the hundreds of hospitals and monasteries run by religious orders during the thirteenth and fourteenth centuries. The hospitals cared not only for the sick, but also for the aged and destitute, including children. Monasteries also performed these functions but in addition there was the daily distribution of food at the gates, shelter for the homeless and lodging at night for the poor traveler, and the occasional caring for and teaching of poor orphans. To some extent, the priests from the monasteries also visited the old and sick in their homes in the parish, bringing small donations of money with them, or more often, relief in kind, such as food, clothing, and fuel. The monastery visitor was the prototype of our present-day concept of the home visitor, the social worker or visiting nurse.

There were those who criticized the almsgiving practices of the monasteries. The indiscriminate giving away of money led to the development of professional beggars and the monasteries were accused of doing nothing more than maintaining the poor that they had made.

The Church's activities for poor relief were supplemented from the twelfth to fifteenth centuries by the craft and merchants' guilds, which supported their own poor and needy. Church, manor, and guild provided relief but made no effort to rehabilitate or alter the abysmal living conditions of the great masses of the people. These patterns of care continued until the middle of the fourteenth century, and then nature intervened to wreak economic disorganization and social chaos upon the land.

In 1348, the dreaded Black Death swept over England from the Continent, killing at least a quarter of the people. This is a conservative estimate and some authorities claim two-thirds of the entire population of England was wiped out in two years. Many of the people left their homes to flee the plague. The many deaths created a labor shortage and the resulting high wages paid by the newly developed woolen industry lured people off the farms and into the cities. The government of Edward III reacted in 1349 with laws to punish vagrants and almsgivers and to keep the laborers "down on the farms." It marked the first poor law passage by the monarchy and, even though aimed primarily at suppressing vagrancy, it was the beginning of radical changes in the assumption of responsibility for poor relief.

During the fourteenth and fifteenth centuries, a greatly strengthened monarchy vied with the landed gentry and the Church for power. Feudalism was on the decline, industry began to appear in towns, and the flow of money to the Church for poor relief dropped off. As the support of the manor and Church for poor relief declined, the government moved to fill the vacuum. Its first efforts were directed at trying to suppress vagrancy and begging. In the mid-fourteenth century, the problem of suppressing vagrancy became firmly welded to the problem of relieving the poor. Ever since then, right up to the present, we can't think about the poor without at the same time referring to vagrants, those poor who would prefer charity to working, or the "welfare cheats."

In 1388, Richard II wrote this distinction into his contribution to the poor laws. A line was drawn between the deserving poor (beggars impotent to serve) and the undeserving poor (beggars able to labor). For the next 150 years, additional legislation reinforced this distinction and imposed ever harsher penalties against vagrants. The laws of 27 Henry VIII (1535)[6] provided for sturdy vagabonds to be whipped, have the upper part of the gristle of their right ears cut off, and, if they still refused to work, to be executed as felons.

Many of the beggars were children. On the theory that if poor children elicited pity in almsgivers, then crippled children would elicit even more pity and thus more money, some parents and adults made a practice of breaking the arms and legs of their children, maiming or otherwise disfiguring them, or encouraging the development of open and running sores on their bodies.

27 Henry VIII provided that children between the ages of five and fourteen caught begging or living in idleness be put to work in husbandry, labor, or other crafts. It gave the power to the governors of the cities and towns to see that this was done. This early form of binding out freed the parish from the responsibility of supporting needy children and also trained the children in self-support for adulthood. Henry further ordered that the impotent poor were to be licensed to beg. Able-bodied beggars were to be punished and forced to work. Henry also confiscated Church lands and secularized the monasteries and hospitals, greatly diminishing the Church's role in poor relief and increasing the role of the government instead.

Edward VI's restrictions of vagrancy in 1547 and 1549 led to the laws of settlement. These provided that itinerant vagrants could be expelled from a town back to their place of birth or to a prior town where they had lived for at least three years, there to be cared for by the local parish. This was the origin of our present theory of settlement, residency requirements, and removal.

Under Elizabeth I in 1562, the Statute of Artificers[7] further regulated the conditions under which children could be bound out in apprenticeship. The next year, in 1563, Elizabeth imposed the first compulsory tax specifically for the relief of the poor and put the government irretrievably on record as having responsibility for caring for those poor who were unable to care for themselves. This principle was reinforced in the landmark legislation of 1572 which set up overseers of the poor to administer the law and take responsibility for poor relief. For the first time, a secular official had complete charge of poor relief.

During the reign of Elizabeth in the 1590's, disaster again struck England, this time in the form of a severe economic depression. Famine and unemployment were rampant. For the first time, the government realized that some of the poor were willing to work but there were no jobs available. To the vagrant and the impotent poor there was now added the genuinely unemployed. (A parallel change in thought about the poor was seen in America during the depression of the 1930's, when people once again discovered that economic conditions might, after all, have something to do with poverty and unemployment.)

The result of the depression was a general overhaul of the poor laws, which were codified in the Statute of 1597, entitled "An Act for the Relief of the Poor." This act pulled together the recent legislative and administrative experience with the poor. The law was amended in small ways four years later, and it is this later revision, the Statute of 43 Elizabeth (1601)[8] that is usually referred to as the "Elizabethan Poor Laws." It was to remain the basic law of the land for the next 250 years and was borrowed by the colonies for their law and it haunts us to the present day.

43 Elizabeth (1601)

The Elizabethan poor laws solidified some of the important issues concerning the poor. It held the local community, the parish, responsible for the support of the poor, provided they had lived there at least three years. It also held that no support had to be given to anyone who had relatives who could support him. (This principle of "family responsibility" for the poor is still a live issue in welfare today, as witness the "man in the house" provisions of welfare eligibility.)

As for dependent children, "43 Elizabeth" established a number of ways of dealing with them. They could be placed out with any citizen willing to take them without charge. If no such person was found, then the child could be auctioned off to the lowest bidder (that is, bids were made to the parish on the cost of caring for the child and the parish chose the lowest bidder — this kept the cost to the parish down but probably didn't markedly improve the child's standard of living).

Another method was devised for children eight years or older who were capable of working. Girls were indentured to a townsman for domestic work until age twenty-one or until they were married. Boys were indentured to a tradesman until their twenty-fourth birthday. The master taught the child his trade and maintained and educated him without cost to the parish.

A third method was for batches of children to be given to manufacturers who required child labor in their factories. Sometimes this was modified as a form of "outdoor relief." The child was allowed to stay with parents or relatives, but was supplied with yarn, wool, or hemp and earned his keep at home industry for a local craftsman or merchant.

If none of these methods worked out, the child went to the poorhouse.

Maintaining the Destitute and Punishing the Idle

Most poor laws were aimed at maintaining the worthy poor while punishing the idler. One other method of English care for children and the poor should be mentioned. Its precise origins in England are not clear, but it was a major method of handling the poor, and, at least in the cities, was in existence in the early 1600's. The method was to place the poor in institutions and two separate types developed based on the two classes of the poor.

For the impotent poor, there were the hospitals, almshouses, or poorhouses. In these places were gathered the old, sick, crippled, blind, mute, insane, and mothers with young children. Almshouses were widely set up in many parishes under a law in 1597.

For the thriftless or vagrants able to work, there were the workhouses. Vagrants and some children alike were forced into labor, supplied with hemp, wool, flax, and iron with which to make clothes and other items. A later form of the workhouse was the House of Correction. These were widely established under legislation in 1576, though the first Bridewell in London probably dates from around 1555. Sometimes both the poorhouse and the workhouse were in the same building, a kind of mixed workhouse.

Around 1700, an experiment was tried in training the inmates of workhouses to manufacture goods for export. Cities trained the adults and child inmates of their workhouses in spinning, weaving, knitting, and manufacturing nets and sails. The products were shoddy and the project collapsed. The unskilled poor could not compete with skilled factory workers. (The same difficulty exists in the United States today in putting the poor to work. The vast majority of the poor are unskilled laborers.)

Some years later, as the industrial revolution began to catch on, another idea for utilizing the poor was developed. Contracts were let with private manufacturers to employ the poor from the workhouses. Anyone who refused to enter the workhouses was denied relief. Some private manufacturers ran their own workhouses as a supply of cheap labor.

There were even a few people who went into the business of operating workhouses, attempting to turn a profit on them. At any rate, the workhouse situation deteriorated to such a marked degree that by the end of the eighteenth century, shortly before the American War for Independence, a workhouse reform movement began in England. One of the needs for such a movement can be seen from the fact that came to light concerning the infant mortality rate in the workhouses. In some of them, as high as 80 to 90 percent of all babies under one year of age died.

Early Practices in the American Colonies

The early methods of care for dependent and neglected children in America, at least until 1800, fell into three major categories. The most important was indenture and apprenticeship. The second method was to maintain children in the American versions of the almshouses. Lastly, there were limited amounts of outdoor (home) relief.

INDENTURE[9]

Indenture was a method of child care widely used in England before the settlement of the New World. It also gained a foothold in America. The example of the indenturing of children by the Virginia Company in the 1620's to its colony in America has already been mentioned. The children were indentured for at least seven years as domestics or farmhands, or apprenticed to a master to learn a trade. At the end of that time (usually twenty-one years of age), they were free, given fifty acres of land and provisions from the company, such as corn, munitions, and a cow.

The English were not the only ones to use this method of populating their colonies. In 1654, the Dutch East India Company sought to increase the population of New Amsterdam (New York City) by sending several hundred children to the colony from the almshouses of Dutch cities.

These children were also bound out as apprentices and household servants for varying periods, usually two to four years. At the end of their indenture, they too were given fifty acres of land. Sometimes there was a cash payment of forty to eighty guilders. The Dutch also sent children to their short-lived colony in Delaware. The colonists advised the company to send them children fifteen years of age or older (which probably accounts for their short terms of indenture), since there was very little chance for profit unless the children could work.

The Dutch colony in New Amsterdam followed the practice of their homeland in appointing orphan-masters to look after the interests of those orphans who had property.[10] They had the power to bind out children. There is a record of a child bound out in such a manner in 1660 for a term of three years. At the end of that time the child had a choice. If he wanted to return to Holland, he was to be given 150 florins. If he elected to stay in the colony, he received two hogsheads of tobacco.[11]

Once the colonies were established, indenture became a method of dealing with the children of colonists who had been orphaned, neglected, or who were illegitimate or poverty-stricken. Shortly after the founding of the colony in Massachusetts, for example, the first child was placed out by public authority. The year was 1636 and the child's name was Benjamin Eaton.[12] He was probably seven years old at the time, since he was given to a widow for a period of fourteen years. Release from indenture in the English colonies was typically twenty-one years of age for males.

Indenture was usually for orphan children without relatives or friends. Poor children with family could sometimes be cared for through home relief, but this was not always the case. The major concern of the colonists was that the child not become a burden to the community. Indenture was a way of cutting public costs and not primarily a way of looking after the child's general welfare, although the colonists probably thought they were meeting the best interests of both child and community.

Poor parents who could not support their children could voluntarily indenture them to others. Sometimes the towns, either believing a child was neglected or sensing that he was about to become a public charge, would issue the parents an ultimatum: either you indenture your child or we'll do it for you. After American independence, New York State passed a law in 1788 which legalized indentures entered into by minors with the consent of their parents or guardians. It also made it possible for children without parents or guardians to bind themselves out with the consent of a judge or justice of the peace. In addition, where the father was absent, it gave the mother the legal right to bind out her children if she so desired. In New York City and Albany, if children were found begging in the streets, the mayor or aldermen could bind them out without the parents' consent.

Children could be bound out at any age up to twenty-one years. There are records of a child being bound out in New York at four years of age in 1726, and the year before that, of a child eighteen months old being indentured. Usually a formal contract of indenture was drawn up and it generally covered the following points. The length of indenture and the date on which the child became free were usually specified. Typically, in the case of males this was twenty-one and for females it was eighteen years of age or until they married.

Even in the very early contracts, there was often a clause concerning education, specifying, for example, that the child had to be taught to read, write, and cipher. Sometimes it was more general, such as the child shall "be sent to school at around 12 years of age for three years." Often the children, especially males, were indentured to learn a particular trade, for example, "to learn the art and mystery of blacksmithing." Other common occupations were: cooper, carpenter, cordwainer, farmer, mason, seaman, clothier; and for girls, housewifery, that is, spinning, weaving, knitting, and sewing.

It was up to the master to pay the costs of keep of the child. The contract usually specified this in a broad way, such as "to provide meat, drink, lodging, apparel and washing." In the more detailed contracts, the apprentice's behavior was detailed: he should keep his master's secrets, protect his property, not play at cards or dice, or commit fornication, or frequent alehouses, et cetera.

The final part of the contract usually dealt with what was due the child at the end of his indenture. This varied from very little to substantial payments. The most generous were probably in the cases where the freed children were being encouraged to become part of an established colony. Otherwise, boys usually received two suits of clothes (one for the Lord's Day and one for working), the girls the same plus a new cloak and a bonnet. In Dutchess County, in New York, in the late 1700's, boys also received a beaver hat, a new Bible, and twenty pounds of York money in cattle or sheep. The girls also received a new Bible plus thirty pounds of good geese feathers. In Pennsylvania, there is a record of a girl receiving clothes as good as she now has (if not better), two heifers with two calves, and a sow with pigs, or with pigs by her side.

The life of an indentured child was often hard. Some masters were cruel and exploited the child. The work of the child was more important than his general welfare. Town officials varied in the degree to which they oversaw the children they had indentured. Some were scrupulous about this; others quite indifferent. If a child were indentured as a seaman, for example, he was often far removed from the ability of anyone to check up on how he was being treated. There were many abuses of the system but probably also many times when it worked out well for the child. One such abuse occurred after a child had earned freedom by having learned a trade during indenture, if the master would not hire him as an assistant, preferring instead to get a new apprentice and thus pay no wages at all. Or the master might prevent the newly freed young man from setting up a shop that would compete with his. Even though the child had learned a trade, he was prevented from practicing it. Later laws were passed to prevent these practices by masters.

Though work was an important part of indenture, it was not specifically for job training. For example, did a child indentured at the age of seven need fourteen years to learn how to be a seaman? Indenture gradually fell into disfavor as other methods of child care developed, but it was still around as recently as the early part of this century. It had changed its character to become "on-the-job training" as part of trade schools, but in some states inmates of state schools for the neglected and dependent were still indentured out as apprentices well into the 1920's. The Children's Bureau did a survey in the early 1900's and found the practice alive and well in the backwoods of Pennsylvania.[13] Children as young as three years old were being indentured out and, when they became free, they were lucky if they got one suit of clothes and five dollars for all those years of work.

THE ALMSHOUSES[14]

Up until the latter part of the nineteenth century, the almshouse was a principal place for care of children in America, as it had also been in England. The first almshouse in the New World appears to have been built by the Dutch in Rensselaerswyck, New York, sometime prior to 1652.[15] This was mainly a retirement home for the elderly poor, and a fairly respectable place as almshouses went. From this start, the almshouse situation went steadily downhill.

The Elizabethan poor laws had delineated at least three classes of poor and had begun to develop separate institutions to deal with each class. America repeated not only the English distinctions between the poor but also like the mother country, the attitudes toward them. The colonists also failed to distinguish between adults and children when it came to the care of the poor.

In theory, anyway, there were the impotent poor, those who could not work because of age or infirmity. For them, America developed the poorhouse. For those unemployed but willing to work, there was the workhouse. The house of industry or the house of employment were other names used for both the workhouse and the poorhouse. Finally, for those who would not work (the unworthy poor, the able-bodied poor, the sturdy beggars, or the valiant rogues, as they were also called), there was the House of Correction. This was really more of a jail for misdemeanors where the inmates were forced to work.

Unfortunately, to add to the confusion, in some localities the House of Correction was called by the name "workhouse." The more general name, almshouse, usually was another name for the poorhouse. Part of the problem was that only very large cities could afford three separate institutions. In the small towns and villages, they made do with one building. This was a mixed workhouse, sheltering the worthy, unworthy, and impotent poor, both adults and children alike. In practice, then, the distinctions between the poor were quite confused and they tended to be lumped together in one catch-all place. A parsimonious resolution to the knotty problem of nosology was achieved by New York City in 1736 when it built its first almshouse. It was officially named "The House of Correction, Workhouse and Poorhouse."

Boston built an almshouse in 1660 for the impotent poor and used it also for the first twenty-two years as a placement for children. In 1668, Virginia erected workhouses for indigent children, taken from equally indigent parents against the parents' will. The children were to be taught useful occupations such as spinning and weaving. Newport, Rhode Island, began an almshouse in 1723.

New York City finished its almshouse in 1736, an imposing two-story building of stone, 24 feet wide and 65 feet long. It was well equipped with four spinning wheels, two wheels for shoemaking, knitting needles, twelve pounds each of flax, wool, and cotton, and five hundred pounds of old junk. It set aside a room as an infirmary — an unusual aspect of almshouses of the times — thus founding the oldest public hospital in the country, since out of this one-room infirmary grew Bellevue Hospital.[16]

In 1743, Massachusetts authorized the union of towns for the support of joint poorhouses. In Philadelphia, an almshouse was built in 1767 and a poor farm in 1773. By 1800, that city was using a newer and larger almshouse, as was also New York City. A county almshouse system began in Maryland in 1768, in Delaware in 1823, and in New York State the following year.[17] In 1769, the town government of Boston, after studying pauperism, authorized five hundred pounds to be spent to set up spinning schools to "learn poor children to spin free of charge."

Almshouses proliferated during the early part of the nineteenth century. At the start of that century there had begun to be mutterings about the cost of welfare. The almshouse was considered to be the most economical way of caring for the poor. That it was also an inexpensive repository for children can be shown by the extensive use made of the almshouse to care for children.

In 1795, of the 622 paupers in the almshouse in New York City, 259, over 40 percent, were children, mostly under nine years of age.[18] In 1821, in the Boston almshouse were 78 sick persons, 77 children, 9 maniacs and idiots, and 155 unclassified inmates, mostly old and decrepit.[19] The average figure for that institution was 100 to 150 children at any one time. In 1823, New York City had 500 children in the Bellevue Almshouse; twenty-five years later the figure had doubled. In 1834, the Boston Almshouse (originally intended to be a workhouse for the able-bodied poor) now contained 134 sick persons, 132 children (104 of school age and 28 at nurse), and a distressing 61 persons insane or idiotic[20] (up from 9 persons 13 years before). It must have been quite an environment for children! At one of the Massachusetts state almshouses, 44 percent of its admissions during the first year of operation were children. At another, 57 percent of its 723 admissions were children.[21] These facilities rapidly became asylums for poor children.

Of course, these figures refer to only part of the total children under care. Some children were on outdoor relief. For example, in Bellevue Almshouse in New York, in 1823, there were 500 children, but there were 4,000 more on outdoor public relief.

A study of the poor in New York State in 1824 found that of those on permanent support, 35 percent were unable to work because of age and infirmity, 27 percent were able to earn a living, and the remaining 38 percent were children under fourteen years of age.

The large population of children in almshouses existed in spite of the very common practice of binding out children from the almshouses whenever possible. Some of the very early factories in America turned to the almshouse children for a source of cheap labor. If you were a citizen of New York City in 1750, you could read in your newspaper notices to the effect that the almshouse had two children, boys, ages eight and ten, waiting for suitable apprenticeships. In 1794, a total of 94 children were bound out from the New York Almshouse.[22] In fact, those bound out may have been the lucky ones.

SCRAWNY, SORE-EYED EXAMPLES OF UNNECESSARY
WRETCHEDNESS

The plight of the children who lived in the almshouses was far from happy. There was no separation of persons by age, sex, or condition. The old, sick, blind, crippled, epileptics, idiots, children, unmarried mothers, tramps, criminals, prostitutes, and the insane were all intermingled. The last category often comprised one-quarter to one-half of the total population. In the words of observers of the day, children were exposed to "disease, perversion and vice." Another reported that the education of children (in the almshouses) was neglected and that they lived in "filth, idleness, ignorance, and disease, to become early candidates for the prison or the grave."

The almshouses were a human scrap heap. The building was often old and in poor repair. Beds were a pile of straw on the floor and sanitary conditions were terrible and sanitary facilities lacking. It is no wonder the children who lived there were described as "scrawny, sore-eyed examples of unnecessary wretchedness."

The "sore-eyed" is a reference to the frequent eye infections that were a scourge in both English and American almshouses. The New York City facility for children moved twice during the 1840's, first to Long Island and then in 1848 to Randall's Island. The reason for the move in each case was an outbreak of ophthalmia. The most likely source of eye infections for children in almshouses was probably venereal disease. One observer describes children being mixed in the almshouse with the "loathsome syphlytic." Sharing the same bed with infected adults and other close physical contacts resulted in the infection of the child. Poor diets and unsanitary living conditions also took their toll. The death rates for children in almshouses began to climb. In some places, admission of children under a year of age to the almshouse was tantamount to signing their death certificate. Between 80 and 90 percent of all the foundlings sent to the Massachusetts almshouse at Tewksbury died there.[23] Death rates ran equally high in other institutions where large numbers of children, with or without adults, were gathered together. Especially vulnerable were the very young children, both to physical diseases and maternal deprivation. At the Foundling's Hospital on Ward's Island in New York City, a total of 1,527 children were received during eleven months of 1868. One year later, all but eighty of these children were dead.[24]

Almshouses remained a major form of care for children during the first three-quarters of the nineteenth century. Very gradually there came about the conviction that they were not the proper place for children and eventually most states passed legislation forbidding the practice. In the meantime, countless children died or were blinded or crippled for life. It was 1875 before New York State passed a law forbidding children to be placed in almshouses for more than sixty days without being accompanied by a parent or relative. It was eight years later before New York, Pennsylvania, and Massachusetts entirely forbade the placing of children aged from two to sixteen in almshouses. By contrast, in England a Royal Commission as early as 1834 recommended the segregation of children from adults in the mixed workhouses.

The Rise of Institutions and Charitable Groups

The practices of indenture and of placing children in almshouses served some positive value. The presence of these
practices and their obvious abuses and shortcomings helped
give impetus to two changes in child care. It led on one
hand to increasing demands for free public schooling and
it gave rise to specialized institutions and charitable groups
concerned with the welfare of children. Child care institutions in America arose out of protest over conditions in
the almshouses and the practice of indenture.

Child care institutions[25] for children had an early but
slow start in America. Prior to 1800, there were only five
private institutions for children in the United States and
only one public institution. By 1923, there were 1,558 such
institutions, but only 8 of these had originated before 1800
and another 93 opened between 1800 and 1850.[26] The last
half of the nineteenth century saw rapid proliferation of
children's institutions, with many starting at the close of
the Civil War as homes for orphans of Civil War soldiers.[27]

Most of the early institutions arose because a specific person or group of people responded to a particular local need.
They were the result of the right person being at the right
place at the right time. The early institutions gave proof
of Emerson's statement that an institution is the lengthened
shadow of one man.

It is generally agreed that the first such institution in
this country was founded by an order of Ursuline nuns in
New Orleans in 1729. The original purpose of the Sisters
had been to provide schooling and religious education to
poor girls. However, on November 29, 1729, a band of
Natchez Indians, angered by French attempts to drive them
from their lands, slaughtered the entire garrison of Fort
Rosalie. Ten daughters of French soldiers massacred by the
Indians were taken into care as a group by the Sisters.

The Sisters continued to care for orphans and other
dependent children until 1912. As late as 1910, they still

had thirty-eight girls under care at their convent. Of course, technically speaking, the institution founded by the Sisters in 1729 was not in the United States at all but in a French colony. It was not until the Louisiana Purchase of 1803 that this area became part of the United States, seventy-four years after the institution's founding. The pattern of child care by religious orders played an important part in places like New Orleans (French) and other future states such as California, Arizona, New Mexico, and Texas, which were under Spanish rule and later Mexican rule. These states did not follow the Elizabethan poor law pattern of care.

The first institutions specifically for children in the colonies proper were probably the earlier-mentioned workhouses for indigent children in the Virginia colony in 1668. Unlike the situation in New Orleans, the motivation for the first institutions for children in America proper grew not out of beneficence, but rather from the concern that children would not be idle but would engage in productive work.

The next institution for children in America came in 1740, in the English debtors' colony of Georgia, only seven years after its settlement in 1733 by General Oglethorpe. The English clergyman, George Whitefield (one of the founders of Methodism), raised the funds for an orphanage called Bethesda (House of Mercy). The home was built ten miles from Savannah, Georgia, and by 1741 Whitefield had forty-nine children under his care. Work was definitely the order of the day here, too, and the children knit, spun, and picked cotton. They were also apprenticed out. The institution survived until 1801, when it split into two homes, one for boys and the other for girls. The girls' home was the first nonsectarian institution founded in the United States (it was run by an independent society formed to promote the work of Bethesda).

The first institution in the country supported by public funds was also located in the South, the Charleston Orphan House, in Charleston, South Carolina. It was founded in 1790. (It would be interesting to know why the South led the way in establishing separate child care institutions.) The city of Charleston led the way with another first, the boarding out of orphaned children in private homes, the first use of boarding home care in the United States. This method was used by the city before the orphanage was built.

It remained for church groups to pioneer institutional child care in the North. In Philadelphia, the Catholics founded St. Joseph's Female Orphan Asylum in 1798. This was the first institution run by the Sisters of Charity, an order which over the years established many institutions for neglected and dependent children throughout the United States.[28] In 1799, the Episcopal church in Baltimore founded a home for destitute girls.

Gradually in the early 1800's, children's institutions began to spring up all over the country. Boston founded an asylum for indigent orphan girls in 1800; New York City opened its facility in 1807; Hartford, Connecticut, in 1819; Cincinnati in 1832; Chicago in 1849; and the Cleveland Protestant Orphan Asylum opened in 1853. Again, it was not a matter of responding to the welfare of children per se as much as it was responding to a local crisis for a particular group of children. Children were orphaned by warfare, by the Indian wars, the War of 1812, the Mexican War, and, much later, the Civil War. There were also epidemics of yellow fever and cholera in the early 1800's that left many children without parents. By and large, the local response to local crises was to be expected, since the country had not yet developed rapid communication and transportation or the widespread cooperation between strong governmental units that could facilitate the more general concern for the welfare of the nation's children.

Of the eight children's institutions begun before 1800 (not all of which survived to the twentieth century) five were founded under religious auspices, two were non-sectarian, and one was publicly supported. In the half century to 1850, a total of 90 other institutions for children were founded, 44 by religious groups, 46 of a nonsectarian nature.[29]

158   *The Illusion of Caring*

The Development of Specialized Children's Charity Groups

The nineteenth century also saw the start of many child
welfare groups, private charitable organizations which arose
to champion the welfare of the poor and of children. Many
of these groups had as their aims the secular and/or religious
education of poor children. In some cases, these groups
naturally evolved to supporting an orphanage, while in other
cases they concentrated on outdoor relief for needy children. The care of the poor, including children, was to a
large extent still a matter of private charity during this
time.[30]

Typical of many such groups was the Ladies Society for
the Relief of Poor Widows with Small Children, founded
in New York City in 1797. A series of yellow fever epidemics
in the 1790's had left many widows and orphans in dire
straits, and the society was formed to help in "the care of
such worthy and respectable widows with small children as
could not provide the means of obtaining even the necessi-
ties of life." [31] The society had very strict standards. It
helped only those mothers who were willing to work, even
if it meant they had to place out their small children as
servants or apprentices; only those who were receiving no
support from the almshouse; only with supplements in kind
to their income (that is, no cash payments); and only those
of good moral character. This latter requirement was not
left to chance; the means, character, and circumstances of
each applicant were thoroughly investigated before any help
was given and aid was denied any who failed to come up
to the good society's high standards. This early form of
outdoor relief or aid to dependent mothers and children
was a good 120 years prior to the mother's allowance law
enacted by the State of New York. During its first year,
the society helped 98 widows with 223 children. Two years
later it was serving 152 widows with 420 children under
twelve years of age. The society proudly reported in one
of its annual reports that its clients would much "rather
eat their own bread, hardly earned, than that of others with
idleness." [32] And work the mothers did. In one year, the

society furnished 3,000 yards of linen for the widows to make into shirts in their own homes.

With its insistence on working mothers, obviously some care had to be given to the small children, and by 1806 the society found itself supporting an orphanage. This orphan asylum was the first institution in New York State for dependent children. It opened in 1806 with twelve full orphans (both parents dead). This was also the first institution in the country to experiment with the small cottage plan rather than the one large dormitory-style institution.

RESCUING MORALLY EXPOSED CHILDREN FROM VICE AND DEGRADATION

These early child welfare agencies went about their tasks with a moralistic fervor, in a single-minded crusade to save children from vice and degradation. Their mission was nowhere better expressed than in the wonderfully old-fashioned names they chose for their societies. The Memorial Home for Girls in Virginia, for example, was an outgrowth of a group founded in 1788 called the Amicable Society. In Hartford, Connecticut, in 1819, the Female Beneficent Society set out to rescue "friendless and indigent little girls." [33] This society later merged with the Hartford Orphan Asylum for Boys, which had been founded in 1833.

In the early 1800's, America saw a period of prolonged economic depression. Later, in the 1830's, there were numerous epidemics that swept over the land. Many of the Protestant orphan asylums in various states date from the aftermaths of cholera epidemics in the 1830's. In the 1840's, the first waves of impoverished immigrants began to pour onto the shores of the promised land. All of these factors created large numbers of poor, orphaned, and needy children. Private societies began to proliferate to meet the many needs of children.

In 1817, in New York City, the Society for the Prevention of Pauperism was formed. It had as a major purpose the "saving of juvenile offenders from vice and poverty." In 1834, the American Female Guardian Society and Home for the Friendless went into action to "prevent crime, diminish the victims of the spoiler, and save the perishing." [34] It founded a home for children and twelve industrial schools in New York City. In Boston, in 1849, the Unitarian church created the Children's Mission to Children of the Destitute. This agency was supported by the contributions of children in the Unitarian Sunday Schools.

One of the most productive and important of the societies was the New York Association for Improving the Condition of the Poor, established in 1843. This group organized the founding of the New York Juvenile Asylum in 1851. Two years later, another offshoot of the group, the Society for the Relief of the Ruptured and Crippled, came into being. The most important contribution of the group came in 1854, when it formed the New York Children's Aid Society. This agency, under its dynamic leader, Charles Loring Brace, initiated a new pattern of child care that set off a major brouhaha the length and breadth of the country. The nature of this conflict will be touched upon in a later section.

Public reaction against the care of children in the almshouses and the practice of indenture led to the founding of children's institutions. The concern of religious and private groups for the religious and secular education of the children of the poor, and for the relief of poverty, led to the founding of many charitable societies during the nineteenth century. In turn, many of these founded orphanages. In general, these institutions were seen as a form of temporary care. Sometimes children from the institutions were placed with private families on a foster home basis. Older children were still indentured out when they reached a suitable age rather than kept in the institutions. Few, if any, of the private societies did direct child placing in families; this was largely the function of the institutions.

Generally, the local and state governments, before the middle of the nineteenth century, were interested in children as the object of public care only by reason of the extreme poverty of their parents or by the children's own delinquency. But gradually the picture began to change. In

Massachusetts, in 1863, a State Board of Charities was organized to supervise all state charitable institutions. One of the first actions of the new board was to recommend the removal of all children from the state almshouses. They advocated finding free homes and placing children in them. Trained supervisors would visit the children in these homes from time to time to ensure they were receiving adequate care. The state institutions were emptied of children and, almost twenty years later, this policy of placing out was extended to all children who came into state care, sidestepping as much as possible the use of institutions entirely. The Massachusetts placing-out system was one of the landmarks in the history of child care. In an 1869 innovation, an agent of the board attended all trials of juvenile delinquents before the courts and he was the forerunner of the juvenile probation officer.

Gradually, some states began to expand their interest in the welfare of children beyond that of poor or delinquent children. The idea developed slowly that the state might just have the right and duty to be concerned with cases of parental neglect or cruelty and abuse. If these things affected the health and education or morals of children, then the state had an interest in these matters. This gradual change in outlook was probably the result of two agencies — the Society for the Prevention of Cruelty to Animals and the Society for the Prevention of Cruelty to Children.

CHILDREN ARE ANIMALS, TOO

The Society for the Prevention of Cruelty to Animals was organized in 1866 in New York City. Its purpose was to look after the welfare of "dumb beasts," to see that horses, oxen, cattle, and dogs were not abused by man. Some eight years later, a church child welfare worker in New York discovered a nine-year-old girl, Mary Ellen, who was being beaten and badly mistreated by her foster parents.[35] The child had been taken from a charitable institution as an infant by the couple that were now mistreating her. The worker was unable to get a court order to remove the child from the home. To the surprise of everyone, it was found that there were no laws in existence to protect a child from abuse.

Greatly disturbed by the mistreatment of the child and the inability of the law to protect her, the worker went to the SPCA for help. After some debate and soul-searching, the society finally decided that since the human child is a member of the animal kingdom, it could act. Legal action was instituted against the foster parents and Mary Ellen had her day in court. The society won the case; the parents went to jail for a year, and Mary Ellen went to live with the church worker who had fought so diligently on her behalf. An important legal precedent was established: "If a child has no rights as a human being under the law, he is at least entitled to the justice of a cur on the streets."[36]

As a result of the successful prosecution of Mary Ellen's case, the SPCA began to receive many complaints of ill-treatment of other children. Hence, in 1875, nine years after the founding of a society for the protection of animals, the Society for the Prevention of Cruelty to Children was created in New York City. Its purpose was "to seek out and to rescue from the dens and slums of the city those little unfortunates whose childish lives are rendered miserable by the constant abuse and cruelties practiced on them by the human brutes who happen to possess the custody or control of them." [37] The society was seen not as a charitable institution but as a subordinate government agency, "the hand of the law, attached to the arm of the law, plucking unfortunate children from atmospheres of poverty and crime." [38]

Societies for the prevention of cruelty to children soon sprung up all over the country. Sometimes animal societies added the protection of children to their functions, while in other places Humane Societies with the dual functions were set up. By 1880, there were 33 societies for the protection of children in the United States. Forty years later there were 57 SPCC's and 307 Humane Societies combining child and animal protection.[39] Their number and importance have declined since World War II, mainly because public agencies have taken over their functions.

Nevertheless, during the time they were in active existence, these agencies did much to see that legislation was adopted protecting children from abuse. One of their first such efforts was directed against the padrone system (the importing into the United States of children who had been sold by their parents in Italy). The early societies were aimed at punishing parents as much as rescuing children.

The problem of child abuse which gave rise to the SPCC's has not been eliminated, certainly not when one to two children a day die in America through abuse from persons society allows to parent. According to one medical source, the number of children under five years of age who are killed by parents is higher than the number of those who die from disease.[40]

GOOD CHRISTIAN HOMES OF THE WRONG FAITH

The dominant position of institutions during the nineteenth century as the major form of child care received a rude shock in the middle of the century. Prior to 1850, child placing in families by noninstitutional organizations was largely unknown. Most placing was done by large institutions with a small number being done by private individuals, and by public officials attempting to rid their communities of dependents. Then a young minister, Charles Loring Brace, changed all of that forever. It was not uncommon for early child welfare workers to have religious backgrounds, but Brace was an unusual minister. He was strongly opposed to indenture and institutional care for children.

Early in the 1850's, Brace worked for the Five Points Mission, bringing the Gospel to the worst of the New York City slums. He worked among the "dangerous classes" of the city, the recent Irish and South German immigrants to America, who happened to be largely Catholics. Distressed by the homeless and vagrant children he encoun-

tered on New York's streets; the ragged young girls with
nowhere to lay their heads; the children driven from drunk-
ards' homes; orphans who slept in stairways; boys cast out
by stepmothers and stepfathers; bootblacks; newsboys;
peddlers; flower sellers and canal boys — all growing up to
enter the adult world of crime, he became determined to
help this motley throng of infantile misery and childish
guilt.[41] In 1853, he helped found the Children's Aid Society
of New York City and became its secretary. The purpose
was to rescue children from the haunts of vice and crime.
Brace's idea of rescue was to ship the children to good Christian homes out West (actually, at that time, anywhere from
northern New York State to the prairie states). The first
year, 54 children were sent to Michigan.[42]

When Brace arrived in a town with his charges, a public
meeting was called, the children were put on display, their
sad histories related, and tearful adults stepped forward to
"adopt" an orphan into their family. Unfortunately, the
good Christians who stepped forward from the West were
Protestants, while most of the children were Catholic. That
didn't bother Brace, who believed that "all differences of
opinion regarding theological and religious belief must be
set aside in the endeavor to secure good homes in which
to place . . . children. The character of these homes is to
be considered, not the denominational sect of the Christian
church which is attended by the family therein."[43] The
Catholics didn't see it that way, and the brouhaha began.

"Perverted fanaticism . . . sectarian zeal . . . coarse pros-
elytization . . . a secret process of routing out early faith and
replacing it with Protestantism," railed his opponents
— none of which deterred Brace. In the first twenty-five
years of the agency's existence, over 51,000 children were
placed out.[44] The religious issue was a continuing contro-
versy and eventually led to the formation of many sectarian
placement agencies and institutions, dedicated to the
preservation of the child's faith (or perhaps the parents'
faith?). It eventually led to charges being leveled against

these agencies that church policies rather than social work considerations determined the treatment that children received from them.

Brace's society was the first non–institution-related child placement agency. His bold creation of a large-scale alternative to institutionalization for the dependent and neglected child launched the beginning of a hundred-year war, between advocates of institutions and those who favored foster homes, over which setting provided the best type of care for children.

This great debate was surely among the most sterile and unprofitable ones in child welfare history. As with many arguments, the form of the question had a lot to do with the sterility of the discussion. To ask simply which is better, foster homes or institutions, is to be led up a blind alley. Perhaps hindsight makes the answer obvious to us now, but one can't help think professionals should have known better than to expect a simple either/or answer. At any rate, there were a number of issues involved in this debate. At first it was a religious one, since children were being placed in foster homes of different religions than their own. As sectarian agencies arose to care for their own, this issue dropped out. Sadly, this trend led to duplication of services, with each group maintaining its own facilities and staff and programs under sectarian auspices.

As the battle was joined, other issues became important. Quite predictably, one centered around public health problems. As mentioned, poor diets, sanitary facilities, and medical care compounded by gathering large numbers of children into one place led to high mortality rates in children's institutions. As late as 1915, 58 percent of all babies admitted to an institution in the western part of New York State died before they were two years old. In the central part of the state, the death rate was 54 percent. In Baltimore, around the same time, of more than 200 foundlings placed in institutions, 90 percent died within a few months.[45] This was a powerful argument for not placing young children in institutions. Today, of course, with advances in public health and medicine, these problems do not exist in well-run children's institutions.

The family has long been viewed as the natural place to raise children and the major vehicle for transmitting culture and social and moral values. To the early proponents of foster home placements, the family setting was the best placement; it was endowed with divine mystique, a quality of "goodness for children" quite independent of the people who comprised the family. It is always difficult to provide satisfactory replies to people who quote divine revelation, and the proponents of institutional care were equally at a loss for words in this argument.

Life at the institution often consisted of monotonous routine. There was little variety in stimulation, little chance to develop independence or establish meaningful emotional relationships with adults. The worst of this type of institution has fortunately disappeared, to be replaced by smaller institutions modeled after family living units. In the better institutions of this type today, there is often a one-to-one staff-to-child ratio. In the small, intensive treatment center, this ratio is often two or three to each child.

It used to be that work played an important part in the life of an institutionalized child. Often the old-style orphanages were self-supporting farming communities. This is not true today, and if children do work in the institution, it is usually for the therapeutic value and not for economic gain to the institution. Staff, which usually were recruited under a patronage system, tend today to be professionally trained child care workers, at least in the better institutions. No longer is it, as it once was, a group of adult misfits caring for a group of child misfits.

Gradually the view came to prevail that institutions were for the long-term care of neglected and dependent children and foster homes for short-term care. Some people felt that long-term care in an institution was harmful to children, that they became institutionalized and unable to function in the "real" world. There was a certain amount of truth to this view, though long-term institutional care doesn't have to be harmful and depends very much on how the institution is run. There is not much doubt that foster home care is cheaper than institutional care and if your main concern is cost, then foster home care will be your choice. This may help to explain why over 90 percent of the children cared for by public agencies in this country are in foster home care.

It is rather clear which side won the debate on how to care for children. It is difficult to say that practice changed because of the debate, though there is no doubt at all that practice did change. In the last fifty years, the trend has definitely been toward foster home care of children and away from institutionalization.

In 1910, for example, of the 176,000 children in foster care, 65 percent of them were in institutions for the neglected, dependent, and emotionally disturbed child. By 1965, with 287,000 children in care, only 28 percent were in child welfare institutions. The projected figure for 1975 is 364,000 children in care with only 17 percent in institutions. The national rate of children in institutions per 1,000 children under eighteen years of age in the total population was 1.1 in 1965 with a projection for 1975 of 0.8.

This national trend is reflected in state statistics. Prior to 1900, New York State had virtually all its children in institutions. By 1910, the figure was still 84 percent, but in 1965 it had sunk to only 28 percent. Massachusetts, an early pioneer in foster family placement, had 49 percent of its children in institutions in 1910 and only 16 percent in 1965. Other states have shown slight increases over the years followed by decreases. Some states still maintain high levels of children in institutions, for example, Tennessee with 65 percent, Kentucky with 62 percent, Georgia with 44 percent.

The other trend that is clear is the relative support of children in institutions or foster family care by agency supervision. In 1965, 78 percent of the children placed in foster family care were under the supervision of public agencies.

By contrast, 86 percent of those in institutions were under the care of voluntary (private) agencies. By 1975, the projected percentages will be: 85 percent in foster family under public auspices and 85 percent of those in institutional care will be under private agencies. By 1975 it is also expected that nearly three-quarters of all the children under both types of foster care will be public charges.[46]

Conclusions and Summary

This appendix has presented a lengthy but by no means comprehensive overview of the patterns of child care for the neglected and dependent child from the Middle Ages to the present. From almshouse to indenture, from orphanages to foster family care, we have seen the problem of the care of dependent children grow out of the problem of dealing with the poor and gradually separate itself from the care of the adult poor. There are many ways of showing concern for children that have not even been touched upon, such as adoption, child labor legislation, and the Social Security Act. This is because our major focus is on the care of children away from their families, primarily those in long-term, impermanent arrangements.

The problem is no longer the care of orphan children. Of all children receiving child welfare services in this country, only about 2 percent have both parents dead.[47] In fact, of the over 70 million children under eighteen years of age in the United States today, only one-tenth of one percent (about 70,000) have lost both parents through death.[48] This is less than one child in a thousand. In 1920, the figure was one child in fifty who had lost both parents through death.[49] The problem is instead the social one of the breakdown of families and, in particular, the care of poor children whose families break down.

The debate about which kind of care is best, foster family care or institutional care, has been resolved temporarily in favor of foster homes. By 1975 it is expected that over 80 percent of the children receiving foster care will be in foster family care. This does not mean it is best. The answer to the question of which is best is that neither is best. Both are needed. The method of caring for a child should be a logical extension of a study of the child's needs. This is at least the theory. In practice, the setting that is chosen for a child is determined by what facilities are available and not by the needs of the child in the majority of cases.

To some in the child welfare field, the institution is the best setting for adolescents trying to break away from parents; emotionally disturbed, acting out, aggressive, or violent children; children unable to form close affective relationships with adults; children whose parents cannot accept "foster family care"; physically handicapped and mentally retarded children; children who have failed one or more foster home placements; children requiring transitory care during acute family crises; and so on. There is also a general axiom in the field that no child under six years of age should ever be placed in an institution.

Other people would include other categories of children in the above list. A few have been mentioned to give a flavor of current thinking. It doesn't matter who is included or who is left out because such a list is so much nonsense. It attempts to treat classes rather than individual children, as if all physically handicapped children were the same. You can find in the literature successful programs that broke each of the above rules. Many of our decisions in child welfare are based firmly upon cherished beliefs and fantasies; they are not rooted in facts.

We know too little about too many things to be dogmatic about anything. There is a great need for research in crucial areas of child welfare and care. Who makes a good foster parent or child care worker? What staffing patterns work best in an institution? How do foster children turn out in adulthood? What alternatives are there to foster care (such as kibbutzim, small group homes, subsidized adoptions, children's bonuses)? There is an even greater need to put into practice the things we already know about what children need to grow up emotionally healthy.

Notes

Chapter 1
1. Proceedings of the White House Conference on the Care of Dependent Children, 9 (1909).
2. Massachusetts General Laws Annotated. ch. 119, sec. 1 (1969).
3. David Fanshel, "The Exit of Children from Foster Care: An Interim Research Report," *Child Welfare*, 65 (February 1971).
   S. Jenkins, "Filial Deprivation in Parents of Children in Foster Care," *Child Welfare*, 8 (January–February 1967).
4. HEW, "The Nation's Youth," Children's Bureau pub. #460 (1968). Other figures are: 85 percent of children under 18 live with two parents (60 million children); 10 percent (6 million children) live only with the mother; less than 1 percent live only with the father (600,000 children); while 3 million (4 percent) live with neither parent.
5. Ibid. Two out of three nonwhite families headed by a woman have incomes under $3,000 and nine out of ten are under $6,000.
6. Joint Commission on Mental Health of Children, *Crisis in Child Mental Health*, 344 (1969).
7. See David Gil, "A Sociocultural Perspective on Child Abuse," *Child Welfare*, 390 (July 1971).
8. Ibid., at 391.
9. *Boston Globe*, 14 (January 24, 1972). The study referred to was probably that done by the Children's Bureau in 1962. For a summary see Morris Paulson and Phillip Blake, "The Physically Abused Child," *Child Welfare*, 86 (February 1969) at pages 88-89. This article is good for general information, giving statistics, incidence data, family descriptions, psychotherapeutic interventions, etc., as well as the author's own study of 96 cases at Los Angeles County General Hospital.
10. This is mentioned not as a criticism of child abuse reporting laws but only to point out that the laws set up an ethical conflict in the doctor which conceivably could lead to his choosing not to report a case of suspected child abuse. The laws place a child's right to safety above the parents' right to protected communications. They are a step in the right direction in that they recognize a child has rights, too, and in some cases these even may be more important than parental rights.
11. Gil, supra note 7, at 390.
12. Sid Ross and Herbert Kupferberg, "Do Parents Own Their Children?" *Parade* (July 27, 1968).
13. *Time*, "The Beaten Generation," 38 (June 12, 1972).
14. Howard James, *Children in Trouble: A National Scandal* (1969); see, for example, pp. 35-37.

172 _The Illusion of Caring_

15. Child Welfare League of America, "The Neglected-Battered Child Syndrome," 41 (1963).
16. Ibid., at 38.
17. In fairness to the public, it should be pointed out that in one recent study, of 1,520 persons over 21 years of age interviewed concerning child abuse, it was concluded that the public was not loath to get involved _indirectly_. When asked what their response would be upon learning that a child had been abused, 47 percent _said_ they would be willing to notify a local welfare agency, and another 23.6 percent _said_ they would notify the police. Only 7.1 percent would keep out of the matter, because they had no business mixing in somebody else's business. (The same study showed only half of the respondents knew about local child protective agencies.)

   If they actually witnessed a child abuse, almost 77 percent of the respondents _said_ they would try in some way to stop the abuse and protect the child; another 20 percent would not interfere themselves but would call the police or a child welfare agency. Only 2.8 percent thought a witnessed child abuse was none of their business.

   From: David Gil, "Public Knowledge, Attitudes and Opinions about Physical Child Abuse in the U.S.," _Child Welfare_, 398–399 (July 1969).
18. Gil, "Sociocultural Perspective," supra note 7, at 392.
19. CWLA, supra note 15, at 36.
20. American Humane Society, "In the Interest of Children — A Century of Progress," 8 (1966).
21. E. Elmer, "Studies of Child Abuse and Infant Accidents," in the Mental Health of the Child, NIMH program reports, 361 (1971).
22. One study of 624 children under the age of 13, who entered foster care for the first time in New York City in 1966, found that only 13 percent of all families in the study consisted of a mother, a father, and a child or children who all lived together before the child or children's placement in foster care! Fathers had been absent from two-thirds of the families for all of the greater part of the children's lives. About one-third of the mothers were single and had never married; another third were not living with their spouse; and 7 percent were divorced.

   Again, this study shows how adults repeat the family situations of their own childhood, for about one-half of the mothers in the study had not themselves been raised by two parents. Twenty-three percent had been brought up only by their mother; 17 percent by persons other than the natural parents; 3 percent by their fathers only; and another 3 percent in foster care.

   See: Shirley Jenkins and Elaine Norman, "Families of Children in Foster Care," _Children_, 156 (July–August 1969).
23. Ibid., at 158.

24. All of the quoted examples of parental comments in this paragraph were taken from S. Jenkins, "Filial Deprivation in Parents of Children in Foster Care," *Children*, 8 (January–February 1967). See also, by the same author: "Separation Experiences of Parents Whose Children Are in Foster Care," *Child Welfare*, 334 (June 1969).

Chapter 2
Relevant to this chapter are the well written and helpful articles by Ner Littner, specifically:
Ner Littner, "Some Traumatic Effects of Separation and Placement," CWLA Pamphlet F-17, 1956.
——, "The Child's Need to Repeat His Past: Some Implications for Placement." In "Changing Needs and Practices in Child Welfare," CWLA Pamphlet F-28, 1960.
——, "The Strains and Stresses on the Child Welfare Worker," CWLA Pamphlet Am-12, 1957.
Sidney Z. Moss, "How Children Feel About Being Placed Away from Home," *Children*, July–August 1966.

Chapter 3
1. Eliezer D. Jaffe, "Effects of Institutionalization on Adolescent, Dependent Children," *Child Welfare*, 70 (February 1969).
2. Robert L. Geiser, "Emotional Readiness to Learn," *Momentum*, 11 (February 1971).
3. Robert L. Geiser, "Some of Our Worst Students Teach," *Catholic School Journal*, 18 (June 1969).
4. Henry S. Maas and Richard E. Engler, Jr., *Children in Need of Parents*, 401, Table 30 (1959).
5. E. A. Weinstein, *The Self-Image of the Foster Child*, 17 (1960).
6. Maas and Engler, supra note 4 at 380.
In addition to those references specifically cited, the following articles were of general background use.
7. Edith Buxbaum, "The Problem of Separation and the Feeling of Identity," *Child Welfare*, 8 (November 1955).
8. In Helen Stone, "Foster Care in Question," CWLA Pamphlet F-38 (1970).
    a. Beatrice L. Garrett, "Developing the Conviction in the Foster Child that He Is Worthwhile," 16.
    b. Norman Herstein, "The Image and the Reality of Foster Care Practice," 169.
    c. Irving Kaufman, "Psychological Costs of Foster Family Care," 250.
    d. Halbert Robinson, "Growing Up Replete," 192.
9. Zira De Fries et al., "Foster Family Care for Disturbed Children: A Nonsentimental View," *Child Welfare*, 73 (February 1965).

Also, the following mimeographed paper, reproduced by the Children's Bureau, HEW, for Child Welfare Staff Training, CW-199B.

10. Almeda R. Jolowicz, "The Hidden Parent: Some Effects of the Concealment of the Parents' Life upon the Child's Use of a Foster Home." From a paper given before the New York State Conference of Social Welfare, N.Y.C., November 1946.

Chapter 4

1. Helen Jeter, "Children, Problems and Services in Child Welfare Programs," HEW, Children's Bureau, 5 (1963).
2. Those interested in pursuing these topics further can begin with the following articles:
   Velma Jordan and William Little, "Early Comments on Single-Parent Adoptive Homes," *Child Welfare*, 536 (November 1966).
   R. G. Andrews, "Permanent Placement of Negro Children Through Quasi-Adoption," *Child Welfare*, 583 (December 1968).
   E. A. Lawder, "Quasi-Adoption," *Children*, 11 (January–February 1966).
   A. Gentile, "Subsidized Adoption in New York: How the Law Works and Some Problems," *Child Welfare*, 576 (December 1970).
   M. Polk, "Maryland's Program of Subsidized Adoptions," *Child Welfare*, 581 (December 1970).
3. Henry Maas and Richard Engler, *Children in Need of Parents* (1959).
4. Ibid., at 356.
5. Henry Maas, "Children in Long-Term Foster Care," *Child Welfare*, 321 (June 1969).
6. David Fanshel, "The Exit of Children from Foster Care: An Interim Research Report," *Child Welfare*, 65 (February 1971).
7. M. Bryce and R. Ehlert, "144 Foster Children," *Child Welfare*, 499 (November 1971).
8. Jeter, supra note 1, at 84.
9. Richard Haitch, "Children in Limbo," *The Nation* (April 1963). See also, by the same author: "Orphans of the Living: The Foster Care Crisis," Public Affairs Committee Pamphlet No. 418 (1968).
10. Joint Commission on Mental Health of Children, *Crisis in Child Mental Health*, 346 (1969).
11. Bryce, supra note 7, at 500, 502.
12. Ibid., at 502.
13. Maas, supra note 5, at 330 (Table 9).
14. Bryce, supra note 7, at 502 (Table III).
15. Maas, supra note 5, at 324 (Table 2). See also, Maas and Engler, supra note 3, at 423 (Table 37).
16. Paul Weinberger and Peggy Smith, "The Disposition of Child Neglect Cases Referred by Caseworkers to a Juvenile Court," *Child Welfare*, 457 (October 1966).

17. Bryce, supra note 7, at 502.
18. Jeter, supra note 1, at 81–82.
19. Fanshel, supra note 6, at 73 (Table 9).
20. Maas, supra note 5, at 328 (Table 6).
21. Ibid., at 328.
22. Alfred Kadushin, "The Legally Adoptable, Unadopted Child," *Child Welfare*, 19 (December 1958).
23. Leon Eisenberg, "The Sins of the Fathers: Urban Decay and Social Pathology," *American Journal of Orthopsychiatry*, 15 (January 1962).
24. Maas and Engler, supra note 3.
25. Fritz Redl, "Crisis in the Children's Field," *American Journal of Orthopsychiatry*, 775 (December 1962).
26. Zira De Fries et al., "Foster Family Care for Disturbed Children: A Nonsentimental View," *Child Welfare*, 73 (February 1965).
27. Draza Kline, "The Validity of Long-Term Foster Family Care Service," *Child Welfare*, 185 (April 1965).
28. See: E. A. Weinstein, *The Self-Image of the Foster Child* (1960).
29. Bernice Madison and Michael Shapiro, "Permanent and Long-Term Foster Family Care as a Planned Service," *Child Welfare*, 131 (March 1970).
30. The size of the literature on any given topic frequently varies inversely with other measures of the importance of that subject. Thus, there is a wealth of information on adoption (which involves less that 5 percent of the children in foster care) but a dearth of information on long-term foster care (which involves over one-half of the children in foster care).
31. M. Wolins and I. Piliavin, "Institution or Foster Family; A Century of Debate," 6–7 (1964).
32. Elizabeth Meier, "Current Circumstances of Former Foster Children," *Child Welfare*, 196 (April 1965). Also: "Adults Who Were Foster Children," *Children*, 16 (January–February 1966).

Chapter 5
1. As quoted in M. Wolins and I. Piliavin, "Institution or Foster Family; A Century of Debate," 19 (1964).
2. R. Chema et al., "Adoptive Placement of the Older Child," *Child Welfare*, 450 (October 1970).
   A. J. Neely, "Adoption by Foster Parents," *Child Welfare*, 163 (March 1968).
   D. Schmidt, "A Commitment to Parenthood," *Child Welfare*, 42 (January 1970).
3. R. Cox and M. James, "Rescue from Limbo: Foster Home Placement for Hospitalized, Physically Disabled Children," *Child Welfare*, 21 (January 1970).
4. N. W. Paget, "Emergency Parent — A Protective Service to Children in Crisis," *Child Welfare*, 403 (July 1967).

5. E. F. Rogan, "The Family Rehabilitation Program," *Child Welfare*, 464 (October 1970).

6. For a summary of the Bureau's work, see the 60th Anniversary Issue of the Children's Bureau in *Children Today* (March–April 1972).

7. Those interested in further information about the Action for Foster Children program should write to: Beatrice L. Garrett, Specialist on Foster Family Services, Office of Child Development, P.O. Box 1182, Washington, D.C., 20013.

8. The League's address is: Child Welfare League of America, 67 Irving Place, N.Y., N.Y. 10003. A list of publications is available upon request.

9. Report of the Joint Commission on Mental Health of Children, *Crisis in Child Mental Health*, 9–25 (1969).

10. Wilbur J. Cohen, "Next Steps for Children," *Child Welfare*, 441 (October 1968).

11. Ibid., at 441.

12. Naomi T. Gray, "Family Planning in the 1970's — A Dynamic Force Affecting the Status of Children," *Child Welfare*, 145 (March 1971).

13. Daniel Thursz, "Can We Insure a Bright Future for Our Children?" *Child Welfare*, 88 (February 1972).

14. Cohen, supra note 10, at 441.

15. Arthur J. Lesser, "Progress in Maternal and Child Health," *Children Today*, 7 and 9 (March–April 1972). See also: United Nations Demographic Yearbook 1970, 648 (1971).

16. Thursz, supra note 13, at 85.

17. Helen Heffernan, " 'There Was a Child Went Forth' — A Philosophy of Early Education," *Child Welfare*, 546 (December 1970).

18. Joint Commission on Mental Health of Children, supra note 9, at 250 and 254.

19. Proceedings of the White House Conference on the Care of Dependent Children, 5 (1909).

20. According to Thursz, supra note 13, at 86, "More social legislation has been enacted by the Congress in the past 5 years than in all the preceding 192 years of this Republic."

21. The Budget of the United States Government, Fiscal Year 1973, 157 (1972).

22. See the article, "Empty Pockets on a Trillion Dollars a Year," *Time*, The Economy, 66–74 (March 13, 1972).

23. Alvin L. Schorr, "Responsibility for Children: What Does It Mean?" *Child Welfare*, 517 (November 1968).

24. Elizabeth Wickenden, "The '67 Amendments: A Giant Step Backward for Child Welfare," *Child Welfare*, 391 (July 1969).

25. *Time*, supra note 22, at 71; also chart on page 72.

26. For a greater discussion of rights and responsibilities under English common law, see: Helen Clarke, *Social Legislation*, 203–241 (1940).

27. Ibid., at 218.

28. Ibid., at 220.
29. Joint Commission on Mental Health of Children, supra note 9, at 3.
30. See the article by Robert Sunley, "Early Nineteenth-Century American Literature on Child Rearing," in M. Mead and M. Wolfenstein, eds., *Childhood in Contemporary Cultures* (1955), p. 159.
31. For a further development of this idea, see: Eda J. LeShan, *The Conspiracy Against Childhood* (1967).
32. Leontine Young, *Wednesday's Children*, 69-74 (1964).
33. HEW, "Dependent Children and Their Families," 24 (1963). Calculations from data provided from this source give about 24 percent of all AFDC children as illegitimate. However, another source (Joe R. Feagin, "God Helps Those Who Help Themselves," *Psychology Today*, 107 [November 1972]) gives the 30 percent figure used here, a more recent estimate based on a 1969 survey of AFDC families in all states.
34. Feagin, supra note 33, at 107.
35. HEW, supra note 33, at 4 and 5.
36. David M. Schneider, *The History of Public Welfare in New York State*, 1609-1866, 213 (1938).
37. Feagin, supra note 33, at 104.
38. Schneider, supra note 36, at 216.
39. As quoted in the editorial, "No Work, No Welfare," in the *Boston Globe*, 10 (January 3, 1972).
40. As quoted in Wickenden, supra note 24, at 391. (No reference source given.)
41. As quoted from an article by Richard Harwood and Laurence Stern, "Welfare work force in U.S. only 50,000," in the *Boston Globe* (January 11, 1970).
42. F. B. Taylor in the *Boston Globe*, 35 (August 17, 1969).
43. Howard James, *Children in Trouble: A National Scandal*, 88 (1969).
44. Harwood and Stern, supra note 41.
45. W. W. Taylor, "Unintended Consequences of the Nixon Welfare Plan," *Social Work*, 15 (October 1970).
46. National Study Service, "Meeting the Problems of People in Massachusetts," 5 (1965).
47. Louis Harris, "Public backs spending on pollution, education," in *Boston Globe* (January 8, 1973).
48. Schneider, supra note 36, at 215.
49. Wickenden, supra note 24.
50. For a further exploration of the public's negative attitudes toward welfare, see: D. J. Kallen and D. Miller, "Public Attitudes Toward Welfare," *Social Work*, 83 (July 1971). See also, H. J. Gans, "The Uses of Poverty: The Poor Pay All," *Social Policy*, 20 (July–August 1971).
51. From Paul Adams et al., *Children's Rights: Toward the Liberation*

of the Child (1971).

52. Heather Ross, "An Experimental Study of the Negative Income Tax," Child Welfare, 563 (December 1970).

53. See Alfred J. Kahn, "The Social Scene and the Planning of Services for Children," Social Work, 3 (July 1962).

Appendix

1. Grace Abbott, The Child and the State, vol. 1, vii (1938).

2. Sanford Katz, When Parents Fail, xiii (1971).

3. Abbott, supra note 1, footnote at 189. See also pages 195-198 for an excerpt from the records of the Virginia Company of London in 1619-1620.

4. England also used this method for getting rid of its adult poor, sick, insane, and convicted prisoners. The English colony founded by General Oglethorpe in Georgia in 1733 was a debtor's colony. The practice of exporting England's undesirables was also a problem for the northern colonies. In 1756, Massachusetts passed a law to keep shipmasters from landing sick and infirm persons on its shores, setting a penalty of 100 pounds for each such offense. See Robert Kelso, The History of Poor Relief in Massachusetts, 56 (1922).

    The practice did not end when the colonies became independent. In 1835, the Governor of Massachusetts protested the unjust and wicked attempt of England to get rid of its burdens by casting them upon the people of Massachusetts (Ibid., footnote 2, at 44). It also was claimed that in 1833 more than half of the population of the almshouses of Boston, New York City, Philadelphia, and Baltimore were foreigners, mostly English and Irish (Ibid., at 43).

5. Material for this section has been drawn from the following sources:
    Helen Clarke, Social Legislation, 398-405 (1940).
    Walter Friedlander, Introduction to Social Welfare, 9-20 (1955).
    Paul A. Kurzman, "Poor Relief in Medieval England: The Forgotten Chapter in the History of Social Welfare," Child Welfare, 495 (November 1970).

6. For an excerpt from 27 Henry VIII (1535), see Abbott, supra note 1, at 91.

7. For greater detail about apprenticeship under the Elizabethan Statute of Artificers, 5 Elizabeth (1562), see Abbott at 91-97.

8. For an excerpt from 43 Elizabeth (1601), see Abbott at 97.

9. Material for this section was drawn primarily from the following sources:
    Abbott, supra note 1, 195-234.
    David Schneider, The History of Public Welfare in New York State, 1609-1866, 16-19 and 75-77 (1938).

10. If the orphans had no property, they were turned over to the poor-relief officials. The issue of children with property was also

a concern for courts in England in the early 1800's. That courts would act only when children had property was rationalized on the grounds that, in the absence of property, the court had no means to exercise its jurisdiction. Since the court could not take on itself the maintenance of all the children in the kingdom, it could only act when there was property that could be used to support the child. (See action involving the Wellesley children as reported in Abbott, supra note 1, at 15, and especially the discussion on this issue at 21–22.)

11. Schneider, supra note 9, at 18.
12. Kelso, supra note 4, at 165.
13. Abbott, supra note 1, at 232–234.
14. Material for this section was drawn primarily from the following:
    Clarke, supra note 5.
    Friedlander, supra note 5.
    Kelso, supra note 4.
    Robert W. Kelso, *The Science of Public Welfare* (1928).
    Schneider, supra note 9.
15. Schneider, supra note 9, at 11.
16. Ibid., 73–75.
17. Clarke, supra note 5, at 170.
18. Schneider, supra note 9, at 181.
19. Kelso (1922), supra note 4, at 173.
20. Kelso (1928), supra note 14, at 200.
21. Kelso (1922), supra note 4, at 174.
22. Schneider, supra note 9, at 181.
23. Kelso (1922), supra note 4, at 179.
24. M. Wolins and I. Piliavin, "Institution or Foster Family; A Century of Debate," 14 (1964).
25. For further information on early child care institutions, see:
    E. O. Lundberg, *Unto the Least of These*, 49–59 (1947).
    J. K. Whittaker, "Colonial Child Care Institutions: Our Heritage of Care," *Child Welfare*, 396 (July 1971).
26. Clarke, supra note 5, at 273.
27. Schneider, supra note 9, at 344. As an example of the effects of the Civil War on orphan population of New York State, Schneider gives the following figures. In 1857, there were 5,403 minor children under 16 years of age in almshouses in the state. In 1861, the figure was 7,962. A year later, in 1862, it had jumped to 24,961 children. At the close of the war, in 1866, there were 26,251 children under 16 years of age in the N.Y.S. almshouses.
28. The religious order of the Sisters of Charity was established in the United States in 1808 by Mother Seton, in Emmitsburg, Md. The order founded and/or took over the management of institutions for dependent and neglected children throughout the United States. The first one they managed, beginning in 1814, was St. Joseph's

Female Orphan Asylum in New York City. In 1817, they were invited to run the Roman Catholic Orphan Asylum of New York. They went on to found and run orphanages in Albany and other New York State cities and towns. Under Mother Seton's direction, Sisters made the long trek by ship to California, to establish orphanages there.

In 1832, the Sisters began operating St. Vincent's Orphanage in Boston, Mass. In 1866, they took over another institution in Boston, the Home for Destitute Catholic Children. This institution moved to new quarters in 1953 and was renamed the Nazareth Child Care Center. It is still managed by the Daughters of Charity of St. Vincent de Paul, as they are now known.

29. Lundberg, supra note 25, at 59.
30. The large, well-endowed private charities and philanthropic associations only became important in the late nineteenth and early twentieth centuries in the United States. They did not play the major role in poor relief that they did in England. This was probably because their development in the New World had to await the amassing of large personal fortunes.
31. Lundberg, supra note 25, at 55.
32. The figures on the Society's caseload in the first few years and the quotation from the annual report are taken from Schneider, supra note 9, at 188.
33. Lundberg, supra note 25, at 57.
34. Ibid., at 71.
35. Ibid., at 103.
36. American Humane Society, "In the Interest of Children — A Century of Progress," 19 (1966).
37. Lundberg, supra note 25, at 103.
38. Ibid., at 104.
39. American Humane Society, supra note 36, at 19.
40. Joint Commission on Mental Health of Children, *Crisis in Child Mental Health*, 344 (1969).
41. Lundberg, supra note 25, at 77.
42. Ibid., at 77.
43. Wolins, supra note 24, at 12.
44. Lundberg, supra note 25, at 77.
45. Martin Wolins, "Licensing and Recent Developments in Foster Care," *Child Welfare*, 571 (December 1968).
46. The statistics in these three paragraphs on the incidence of children in institutions and foster family care were taken from two sources. Those referring to years prior to 1933 came from Wolins (1964), supra note 24, at 36–47, and those from 1933 on were taken either directly or by computation from the pamphlet by Seth Low, "Foster Care of Children — Major National Trends and Prospects," HEW, Children's Bureau (1966).

47. Helen Jeter, "Children, Problems and Services in Child Welfare Programs," HEW, Children's Bureau, 131 (1963).
48. Richard Haitch, "Orphans of the Living: The Foster Care Crisis," Public Affairs Committee Pamphlet #418, 1 (1968).
49. Child Welfare League of America, "Children in Need of Parents," 17 (no publication date given, but probably around 1960, following publication of the book of the same name by Maas and Engler in 1959).
50. These figures on the number of child welfare institutions and foster family homes in the United States were taken from: HEW, Children's Bureau Statistical Series 92, Child Welfare Statistics, 1967 (1968).

Index